INTRODUCTION

Italian food is some of the most delicious and varied in the world, so little wonder it's also one of the most popular. What's not to love about a place that invented pizza, lasagne and tiramisu? *Chop, Sizzle, Wow* shows you how to recreate some of Italy's favourite dishes; it's a cool, comic-strip version of *The Silver Spoon*, a collection of recipes that was first published in Italy in 1950 and has pretty much been the bible of Italian cookery ever since. Like the Bible, it is very, very long so we've picked out the best of the best. These fifty fast and simple recipes are all illustrated to show you, step by step, how to whip up an Italian feast at home.

HOW TO EAT THE ITALIAN WAY

To understand Italian food, you first need to understand Italians and what food means to them. They don't just love food; it is an art form, their 'other' religion. You've only got to listen to a conversation in Italy — be it between people in the countryside or the city — to know that the main topic of discussion is what they'll be having for breakfast, lunch or dinner, and where they'll be going to get it. In short, Italy is a nation obsessed with food, to the point of being fanatical.

Not so long ago, a well-known pasta manufacturer issued a list of 'rules' to help teach foreigners how to avoid messing up when in Italy. It was all food-related of course, and it all came down to keeping things authentic. Why change something that is perfect in the first place? The first crime, unsurprisingly, is putting ketchup on pasta. This is viewed as one of the greatest 'culinary sins', right up there with serving pasta like a vegetable or side dish. Pasta is something to be honoured; the main event, if you will. It should come after *antipasti* (little appetizers) as *il primo* (the first course), and never *il secondo* (the second course, which would be meat, fish or even just vegetables). After that, you might also have *insalata* (a salad course), *formaggi e frutta* (cheese and fresh seasonal fruit, always peeled) and *dolce* (dessert). Other sins include the combination of chicken and pasta, a major no-no — though it's unclear exactly why, the Italians just wouldn't do it — and a ban on adding oil to boiling water for pasta (it should be drizzled, in scant amounts, onto pasta after it's cooked to keep it moist and supple). Finally, what is probably the most important rule of all: eating should never, ever be done alone. Italians believe the only way to show true respect for tradition, food and the art that has gone into making it, is by sharing it with those you love most.

You've probably guessed by now that mealtime in Italy is a sacred affair. Having plenty of time to savour it — two to three hours at least — is essential to fully appreciate every flavour and skill that has gone into putting the food on your plate. That Italians still place so much importance on breaking bread together is the key to their passion for the *dolce vita* (a sweet and happy life) and is also the underlying intent of *Chop, Sizzle, Wow*. The food you make will never taste as good as when you share it with family and friends.

LANDSCAPE AND CLIMATE

The huge variety of Italian dishes comes down to the country's immensely varied landscape and climate, and the fact that Italy wasn't a unified country until the early nineteenth century. Until then, each of the twenty regions we know today was effectively its own little country, brimming with unique flavours born out of having dramatically different environments. Italy is shaped like a long boot with a stiletto heel at the bottom. The top of the boot opens to the snowy, mountainous north, with its deep green pastures and borders with France, Switzerland, Austria and Slovenia. This region produces excellent dairy and meat products, while the hot, arid plains of the southern heel reach deep into the Mediterranean Sea towards Tunisia and are perfect for fruit orchards, tomatoes and olive groves. In the centre the more temperate plains are the country's bread basket, where wheat, corn and barley flourish.

When you put all these products together it's easy to see that real Italian cooking is still a largely artisan affair. It is based on prime, seasonal and local ingredients – never try to fob an Italian off with a tomato in February, or anything less than spring lamb (*agnello*) for Easter – and the majority of dishes are solid, hearty creations designed to nourish the body and nurture the soul. Have you ever noticed the general lack of Italian chefs and cooks fiddling around with foam and liquid nitrogen? That's because they are far too busy sniffing out the best produce in local markets, or hanging out in the kitchen cooking and eating with their friends, or travelling the length and breadth of their country in search of the best Grilled Sardines (p. 58), Steak Pizzaiola (p. 52) or a perfectly made espresso, which, by the way, most Italians agree you'll find in Rome.

KEY INGREDIENTS

It comes as little surprise, then, to discover that each region has edible treasures that make it famous. Emilia-

Romagna, for example, is known for its strong, salty, raw cow's-milk cheese *Parmigiano-Reggiano* (Parmesan in English), Parma ham, and balsamic vinegar so rich and sweet you could almost drink it by the glass. Piedmont is famed for its fairy-tale oak, beech and hazel forests that hide pungent, knobbly white truffles that are among the most expensive ingredients on earth (casino owner Stanley Ho reportedly paid $330,000 for two weighing a kilo each in 2010). Sicily, the biggest island in the Mediterranean, is the place to go for a pleasingly bitter, yet delightfully sweet, blood orange *granita* (like a grainy sorbet, see pp. 82–83 for how to make Strawberry or Apricot Granita) and decadent Cannoli (sweet pastry shells filled with ricotta, pp. 90–91). Tuscan olive oil is so sought-after that food criminals have been known to fake it. Products like these cause Italian hearts

9

to break when they can't get them and chests to swell with pride when they can, and nearly all are protected by the DOP (*Denominazione di Origine Protetta*) stamp of quality. Look out for it when shopping for Italian ingredients. Otherwise, make like an Italian and swap the supermarket for farmers' markets, greengrocers and delicatessens. The quality is usually higher, it's often cheaper and the staff will happily tell you which fruit and vegetables are in season and therefore what is tastiest. Better yet, most places will let you try a little nibble of something before you buy it, making shopping a whole lot more fun (and tasty!).

It won't be long before you learn what Italians have long known: when you can't be bothered to cook, just serve a plate of cheese (combine ricotta drizzled with truffle oil, mozzarella layered with tomatoes and basil, and add gorgonzola for something strong and blue), *salumi* (preserved meats; try thin slices of salami, prosciutto and bresaola), good bread and olives, and dinner is not only done, it's absolutely delicious. And nothing makes people happier than that.

REGIONAL DISHES

Sometimes it's time to get down to some serious cooking. *Chop, Sizzle, Wow* is split into chapters that cover appetizers (*antipasti*), pasta (*il primo*), main courses (*il secondo*), and desserts (*dolce*) to help you put together the ultimate Italian feast. The recipe selection focuses on the most celebrated dishes of different regions.

Florence is king for its one-pot, hunter's style Chicken Cacciatore (p. 60). Naples is home to the classic Pizza Margherita (pp. 20–21), consisting of nothing more than a disc of flat, chewy dough topped with fresh tomato sauce and mozzarella, baked in a hot oven then strewn with fresh basil leaves. Legend has it that it was created in 1889 to honour the visiting Queen Margherita, who insisted that everything that passed her lips resemble the Italian flag! Tucked into the heel of Italy, Puglia is known for its stuffed Panzarotti (pp. 26–27), which look like Cornish pasties and make excellent picnic food. The best Tagliatelle with Peas and Ham (p. 38) comes from Emilia-Romagna; while Carbonara (p. 41), only genuine when served with spaghetti, is a Roman dish. The classic Fritto Misto (pp. 66–67) is at its very best when using seafood hauled fresh from the lagoons of Venice. Twice-baked almond biscuits known as Cantucci (p. 74), called 'coffee bread' in English because they are so good for dipping, are the medieval treasure of Prato; and creamy Pannacotta with Hazelnut Sauce (pp. 78–79) is a treat from Piedmont, where the cooler climate makes for thick forests and lush green grass for better dairy cows. You could spend a lifetime cooking your way through the regional dishes of Italy and never get to the end, but *Chop, Sizzle, Wow* is a great way to start.

SHOPPING TIPS

When buying basic ingredients, keep it simple. You don't need to go in search of fresh pasta – most Italians prefer to use a good brand of dried pasta such as De Cecco – but do invest in good quality olive oil and balsamic vinegar to keep at hand. Canned Italian tomatoes will almost certainly be better than any fresh ones you can buy out of season, but fresh herbs like basil, oregano and sage will give your cooking a bright and lively finish that you cannot achieve with the dried versions. Ready-cooked canned beans these days are almost as good as dried and reconstituted, but fresh fish is always better than frozen and a butcher will ensure you get the right cut of meat rather than you trying to find it in a supermarket refrigerator. If any recipe calls for wine, it can easily be replaced with stock or even plain old tap water.

COOKING AND TECHNIQUES

Luckily, because Italian food on the whole is so practical and down-to-earth, you won't need too much by way of special equipment. Sharp knives are essential, as are chopping boards, wooden spoons and a hand-held balloon whisk. Find a thick-bottomed pan for making risottos, a large

pan for boiling pasta in plenty of water, or heating oil for frying, and a large shallow pan for cooking sauces. Invest in a solid baking sheet for roasting and (when it's turned upside down) for using as a pizza stone in a very hot oven. Add scales, a measuring jug, a cake tin, a set of ramekins, and a couple of mixing bowls

that can double as vessels for salads or desserts like tiramisu, and you're away.

The most important thing when cooking is to read the recipe thoroughly at the very start so you have an overview of everything you need to do. Then set your *mise en place* – that's chef talk for getting all the equipment together and your ingredients weighed and laid out ready for cooking. Heating the oven in advance, or having a bowl of iced water on hand to stop vegetables cooking can make all the difference between success and failure. Once you start cooking, don't forget to taste your food – there's absolutely no other way to know if it needs more seasoning, herbs or spices. But go easy, especially in the case of salt; remember it's easy to add more but impossible to take it away. When serving hot food, warm the plates in the bottom of the oven, likewise the serving dishes if your guests are going to help themselves at the table. For specifics on carrying out certain techniques, such as cleaning fish, see Techniques in Detail, p. 95.

Armed with these basics, you'll soon be turning out food with the ease of a pro – antipasti of Tomato Bruschetta (p. 22) and Sweet-and-Sour Caponata (p. 16), classic pasta dishes such as Linguine with Pesto (p. 46), main courses like Spare Ribs with Polenta (p. 56), and irresistible desserts such as Raspberry Semifreddo (p. 75) and Tiramisu (p. 77), which are perfect for sharing with family and friends. You'll be able to create your very own *dolce vita*.

Buon appetito a tutti!

1 ONION

2 SLICES BREAD

1 CLOVE GARLIC

1 SPRIG PARSLEY

2 TBSP OLIVE OIL

8 PORCINI MUSHROOMS

2 SALTED ANCHOVY FILLETS

1 EGG

4 TBSP BREADCRUMBS

STUFFED PORCINI MUSHROOMS

SERVES 4   PREP: 40 MIN   COOK: 20 MIN

PREHEAT OVEN TO 160°C/GAS MARK 3

FINELY SLICE

CHOP

REMOVE CRUSTS AND SOAK IN COLD WATER FOR 10 MIN

LIGHTLY BEAT

REMOVE CAPS AND RESERVE STEMS

5 MIN IN OVEN THEN REMOVE

KEEP THE OVEN ON AND INCREASE HEAT TO 180°C/ GAS MARK 4

TRANSFER CAPS TO A PLATE

DISCARD WAX PAPER

LINE A BAKING SHEET WITH WAX PAPER

BRUSH SHEET WITH OIL

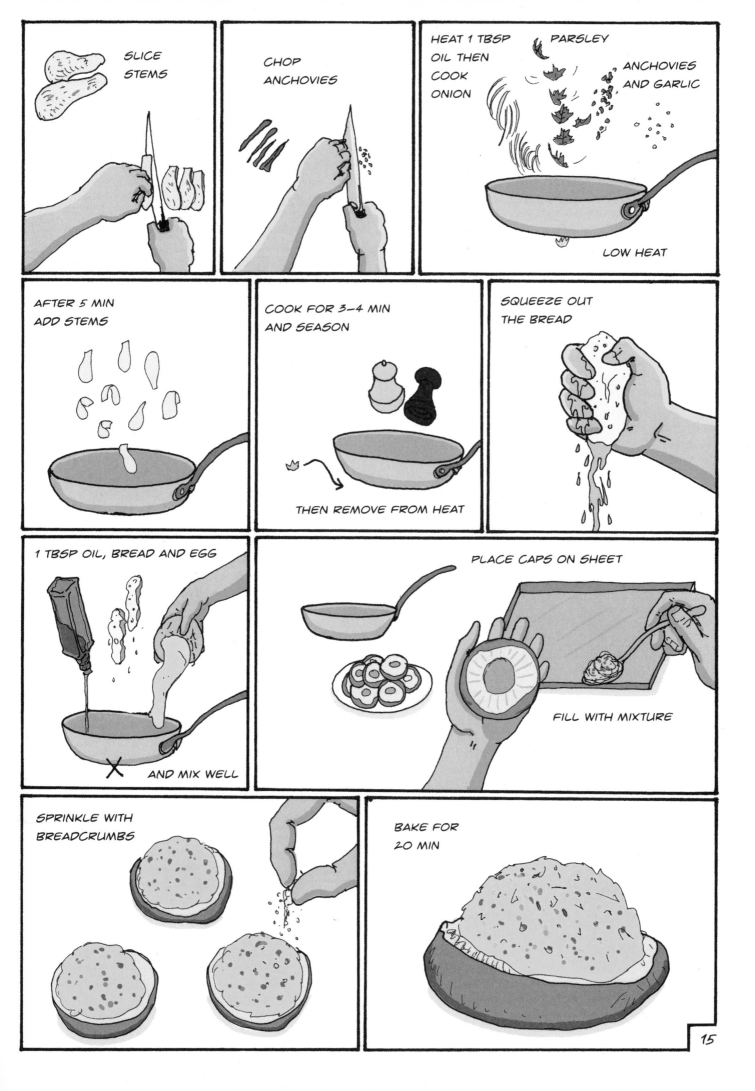

SWEET-AND-SOUR CAPONATA

4 SQUID

1 SPRIG PARSLEY

½ CLOVE GARLIC

LEMON WEDGES

50 G/2 OZ BREADCRUMBS

OLIVE OIL, FOR DRIZZLING AND BRUSHING

GRILLED STUFFED SQUID

SERVES 4

PREP: 30 MIN

COOK: 10 MIN

REMOVE MOUTH AND SET ASIDE

REMOVE HEADS AND INNARDS

THEN SLIDE BONE OFF

PEEL SKIN AND TAIL

GENTLY RINSE

PAT DRY

SQUID MOUTH + PARSLEY + GARLIC

CHOP

ADD BREADCRUMBS, A DRIZZLE OF OIL

SEASON...

...AND MIX WELL

THEN SPOON THE MIXTURE INTO THE SQUID

INSERT A COCKTAIL STICK...

...AND SECURE

BRUSH WITH OIL

AND SEASON

SLOWLY HEAT GRILL

TURN UNTIL GOLDEN BROWN & TENDER

SERVE WITH LEMON WEDGES

ROLLED PEPPERS

4 PEPPERS

1 TOMATO

300 G/11 OZ CANNED TUNA

10 STONED BLACK OLIVES

1 RED CHILLI, CHOPPED

3/4 TBSP LEMON JUICE

FRESH BASIL

1 TBSP OLIVE OIL

SERVES 4   PREP: 15 MIN   COOK: 10 MIN

GRILL PEPPERS UNTIL CHARRED AND BLACKENED

PLACE IN A PLASTIC BAG, TIE THE TOP AND LEAVE TO COOL

PEEL OFF THE SKINS

DRAIN TUNA

BLANCH TOMATOES

BOILING WATER

ICED WATER

PEEL

CHOP

DE-SEED PEPPERS

AND CUT INTO 2-3 LARGE SLICES

TUNA   TOMATOES   BASIL

OLIVES   CHILLI

PROCESS

ADD LEMON JUICE AND OLIVE OIL

SPREAD ONTO PEPPER SLICES

ROLL UP

LET COOL BEFORE SERVING

18

4 SMALL SLICES
BACON FAT (LARDO)

4 EGGS

4 TBSP
DOUBLE CREAM

2 TBSP
PARMESAN
(WHEN GRATED)

EGGS EN COCOTTE

SERVES 4   PREP: 10 MIN   COOK: 6–8 MIN

PREHEAT OVEN
TO 180°C/
GAS MARK 4

PARBOIL FOR
1 MIN

PUT
1 SLICE
BACON
FAT AND

1 TBSP
CREAM
IN EACH
RAMEKIN

PLACE RAMEKINS
IN ROASTING PAN

POUR IN
BOILING
WATER
TO HALF
WAY UP
RAMEKINS

Bake

FOR 6–8 MIN

THE COMBINATION
OF STRONG AND
SAVOURY BACON
FAT WITH THE MILD
TASTE OF CREAM
GIVES THE EGGS A
DELICATE FLAVOUR

120 ML/4 FL OZ LUKEWARM WATER

OLIVE OIL, FOR DRIZZLING

150 G/5 OZ MOZZARELLA CHEESE

250 G/9 OZ PLAIN FLOUR

5–6 TOMATOES

11 G/⅓ OZ FRESH YEAST

6 BASIL LEAVES

PIZZA MARGHERITA

SERVES 4   PREP: 1½ HR   COOK: 25 MIN

SIFT FLOUR AND PINCH SALT

MASH FRESH YEAST WITH THE WATER

MAKE A WELL IN THE FLOUR AND POUR IN THE YEAST MIXTURE

GENTLY STIR

UNTIL SOFT AND NOT TOO STICKY

AND ON A FLOURED SURFACE... ...KNEAD FOR 10 MIN OR UNTIL SMOOTH AND ELASTIC

SHAPE INTO A BALL

COVER WITH OILED CLINGFILM

LET RISE IN A WARM PLACE FOR 1 HR UNTIL DOUBLED IN SIZE

Margherita

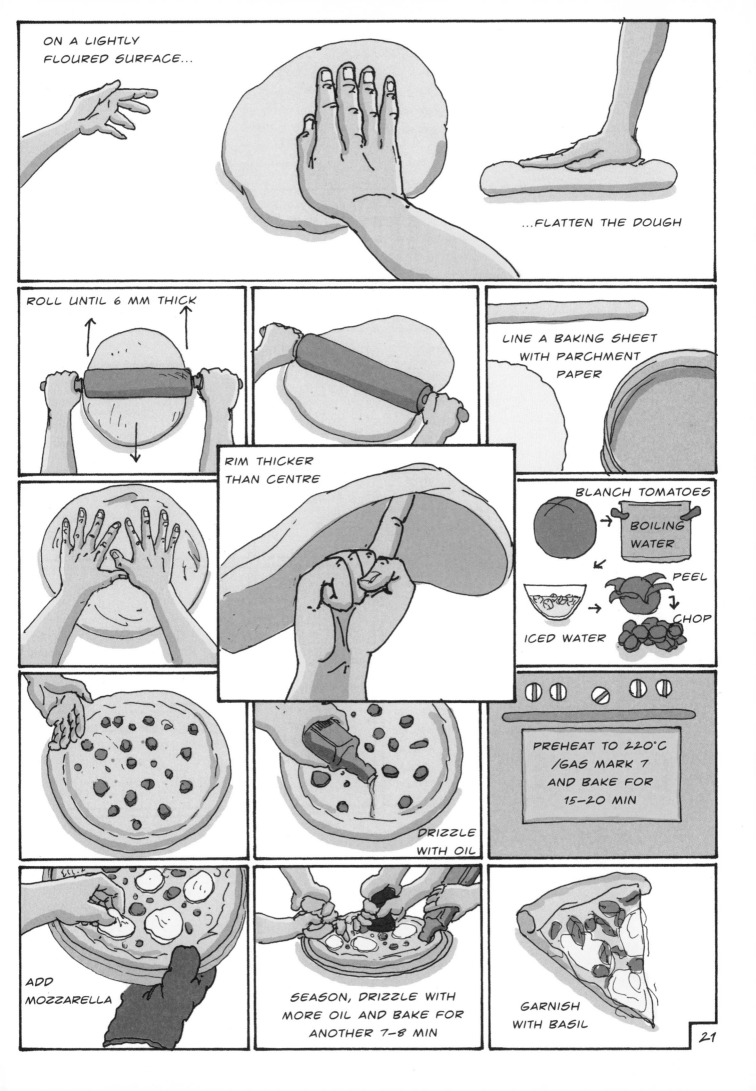

ON A LIGHTLY FLOURED SURFACE...

...FLATTEN THE DOUGH

ROLL UNTIL 6 MM THICK

LINE A BAKING SHEET WITH PARCHMENT PAPER

RIM THICKER THAN CENTRE

BLANCH TOMATOES

BOILING WATER

ICED WATER

PEEL

CHOP

DRIZZLE WITH OIL

PREHEAT TO 220°C /GAS MARK 7 AND BAKE FOR 15-20 MIN

ADD MOZZARELLA

SEASON, DRIZZLE WITH MORE OIL AND BAKE FOR ANOTHER 7-8 MIN

GARNISH WITH BASIL

RUSTIC (COUNTRY-STYLE) LOAF

4 GARLIC CLOVES

6-8 PLUM TOMATOES

EXTRA-VIRGIN OLIVE OIL

TOMATO BRUSCHETTA

SERVES: 4   PREP: 20 MIN   COOKING: 5 MIN

Dice

PREHEATED GRILL

TOAST ONE SIDE

THEN THE OTHER

RUB WITH GARLIC WHILE STILL HOT

PUT BACK UNDER THE GRILL FOR A MOMENT.

TOP WITH TOMATOES

SEASON

AND DRIZZLE WITH OIL

ALTERNATIVE BRUSCHETTA TOPPINGS ARE:

MOZZARELLA, PROSCIUTTO, ANCHOVIES, BROAD BEANS, BASIL

22

POTATO CROQUETTES

Ingredients:
- 800 G/1¾ LB FLOURY POTATOES
- 100 G/3½ OZ FONTINA CHEESE
- 1 SPRIG BASIL
- 50 G/2 OZ COOKED HAM
- 3 EGGS
- VEGETABLE OIL
- 50 G/2 OZ PARMESAN CHEESE
- 80 G/3 OZ BREADCRUMBS

SERVES 4　　PREP: 1 1/2 HR　　30–40 MIN

COOK FOR 45 MIN — SALTED BOILING WATER

GRATE PARMESAN

HAM — CUT INTO STICKS — FONTINA

PEEL AND MASH THE POTATOES

ADD 1 EGG AND 1 YOLK TO THE POTATOES

THEN ADD PARMESAN, SEASON AND MIX

SHAPE

PUSH A STICK OF HAM AND FONTINA INTO EACH CROQUETTE

BEATEN EGG — BREADCRUMBS

HEAT OIL IN A DEEP PAN TO 180°C OR UNTIL A CUBE OF BREAD BROWNS IN 30 SEC AND FRY CROQUETTES UNTIL GOLDEN

GARNISH WITH BASIL

23

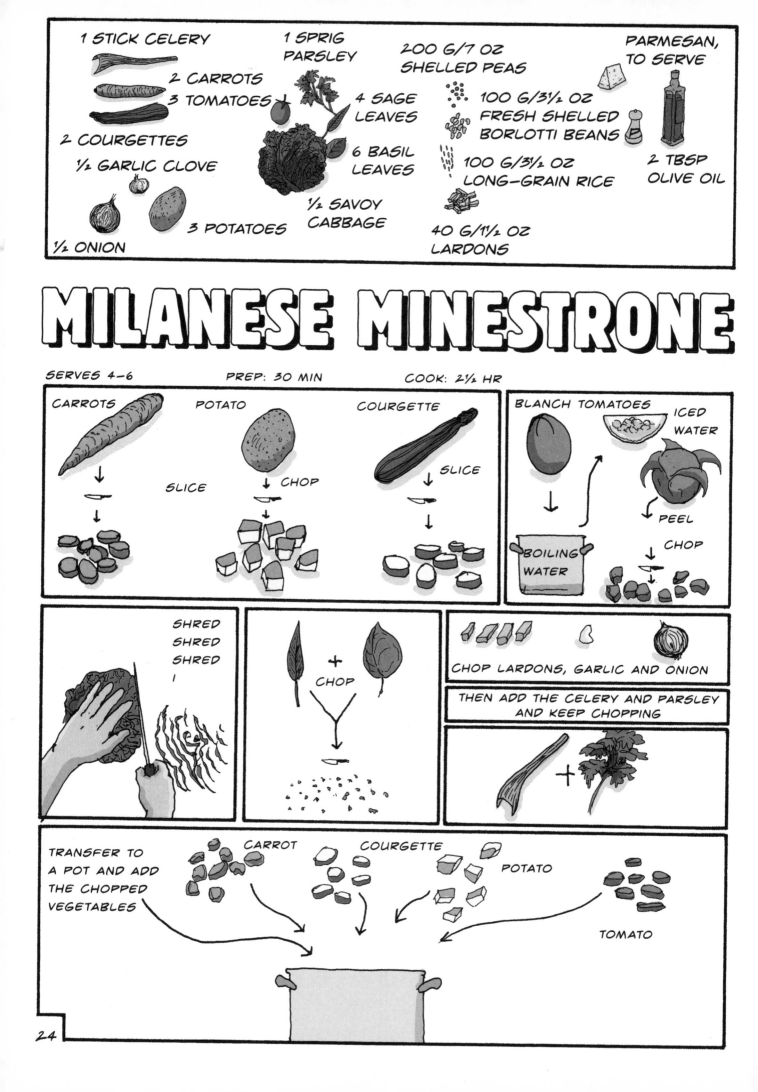

MILANESE MINESTRONE

Ingredients:
- 1 STICK CELERY
- 2 CARROTS
- 3 TOMATOES
- 2 COURGETTES
- ½ GARLIC CLOVE
- ½ ONION
- 3 POTATOES
- 1 SPRIG PARSLEY
- 4 SAGE LEAVES
- 6 BASIL LEAVES
- ½ SAVOY CABBAGE
- 200 G/7 OZ SHELLED PEAS
- 100 G/3½ OZ FRESH SHELLED BORLOTTI BEANS
- 100 G/3½ OZ LONG-GRAIN RICE
- 40 G/1½ OZ LARDONS
- PARMESAN, TO SERVE
- 2 TBSP OLIVE OIL

SERVES 4–6   PREP: 30 MIN   COOK: 2½ HR

CARROTS — SLICE

POTATO — SLICE ↓ CHOP

COURGETTE — SLICE

BLANCH TOMATOES — BOILING WATER — ICED WATER — PEEL — CHOP

SHRED SHRED SHRED !

CHOP

CHOP LARDONS, GARLIC AND ONION

THEN ADD THE CELERY AND PARSLEY AND KEEP CHOPPING

TRANSFER TO A POT AND ADD THE CHOPPED VEGETABLES — CARROT — COURGETTE — POTATO — TOMATO

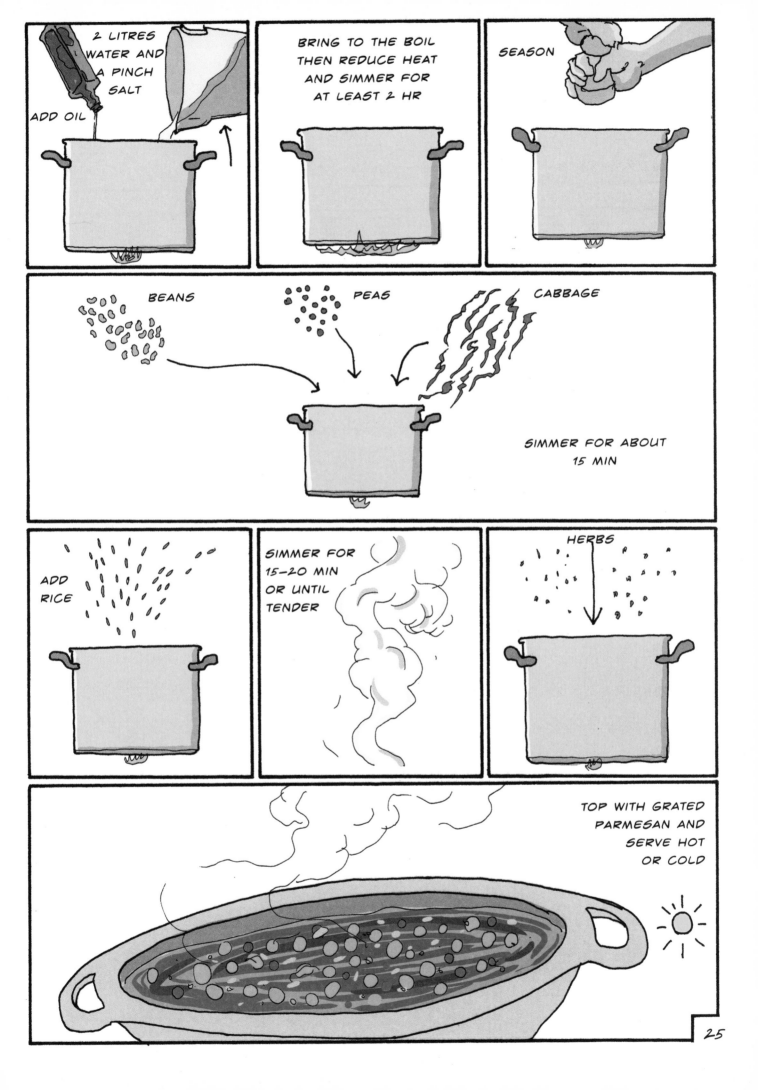

25

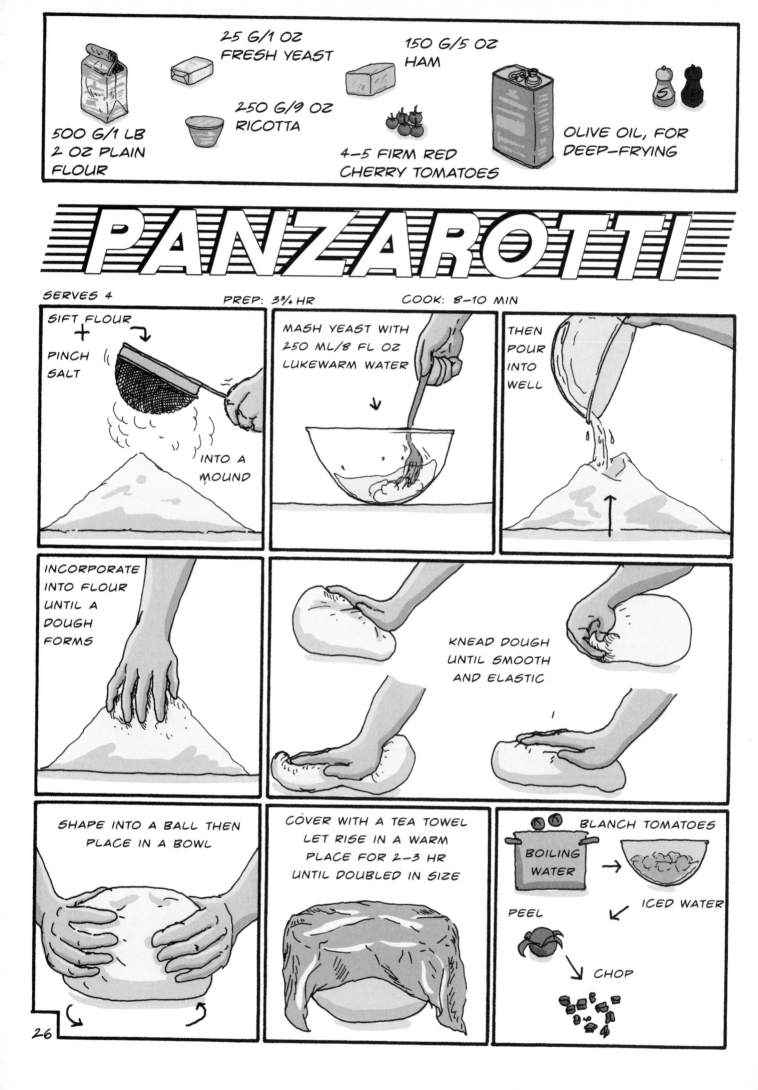

PANZAROTTI

Ingredients:
- 500 G/1 LB 2 OZ PLAIN FLOUR
- 25 G/1 OZ FRESH YEAST
- 250 G/9 OZ RICOTTA
- 150 G/5 OZ HAM
- 4–5 FIRM RED CHERRY TOMATOES
- OLIVE OIL, FOR DEEP-FRYING

SERVES 4   PREP: 3¾ HR   COOK: 8–10 MIN

SIFT FLOUR + PINCH SALT INTO A MOUND

MASH YEAST WITH 250 ML/8 FL OZ LUKEWARM WATER

THEN POUR INTO WELL

INCORPORATE INTO FLOUR UNTIL A DOUGH FORMS

KNEAD DOUGH UNTIL SMOOTH AND ELASTIC

SHAPE INTO A BALL THEN PLACE IN A BOWL

COVER WITH A TEA TOWEL LET RISE IN A WARM PLACE FOR 2–3 HR UNTIL DOUBLED IN SIZE

BLANCH TOMATOES
BOILING WATER
ICED WATER
PEEL
CHOP

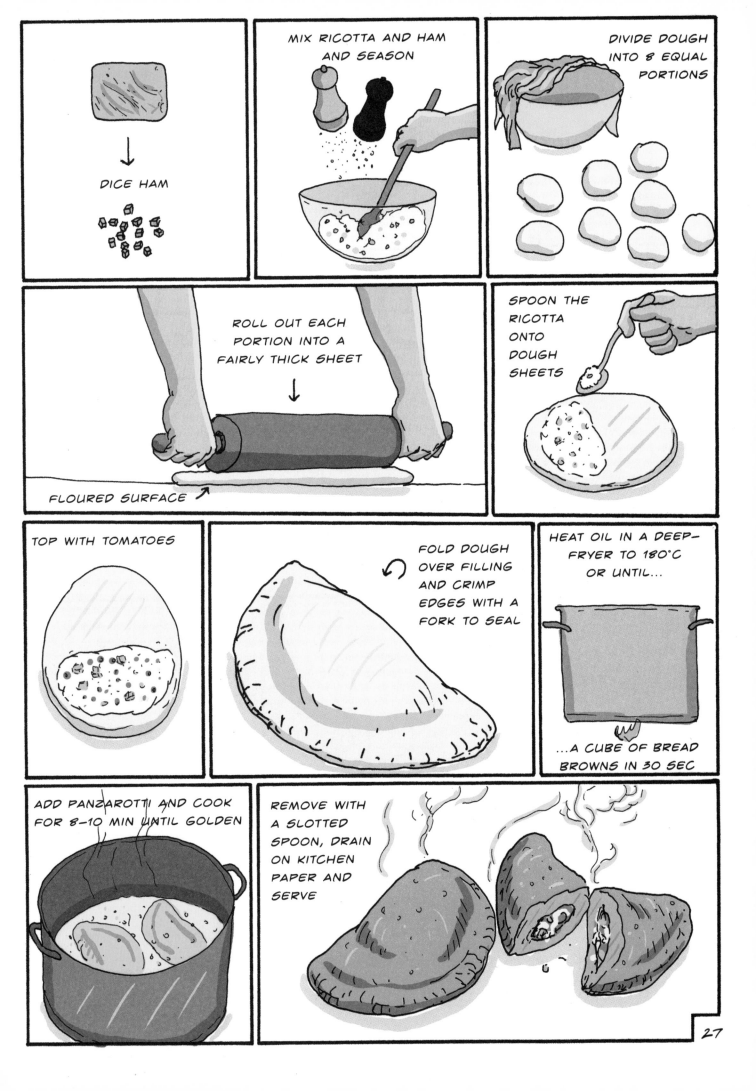

DICE HAM

MIX RICOTTA AND HAM AND SEASON

DIVIDE DOUGH INTO 8 EQUAL PORTIONS

ROLL OUT EACH PORTION INTO A FAIRLY THICK SHEET

FLOURED SURFACE

SPOON THE RICOTTA ONTO DOUGH SHEETS

TOP WITH TOMATOES

FOLD DOUGH OVER FILLING AND CRIMP EDGES WITH A FORK TO SEAL

HEAT OIL IN A DEEP-FRYER TO 180°C OR UNTIL...

...A CUBE OF BREAD BROWNS IN 30 SEC

ADD PANZAROTTI AND COOK FOR 8-10 MIN UNTIL GOLDEN

REMOVE WITH A SLOTTED SPOON, DRAIN ON KITCHEN PAPER AND SERVE

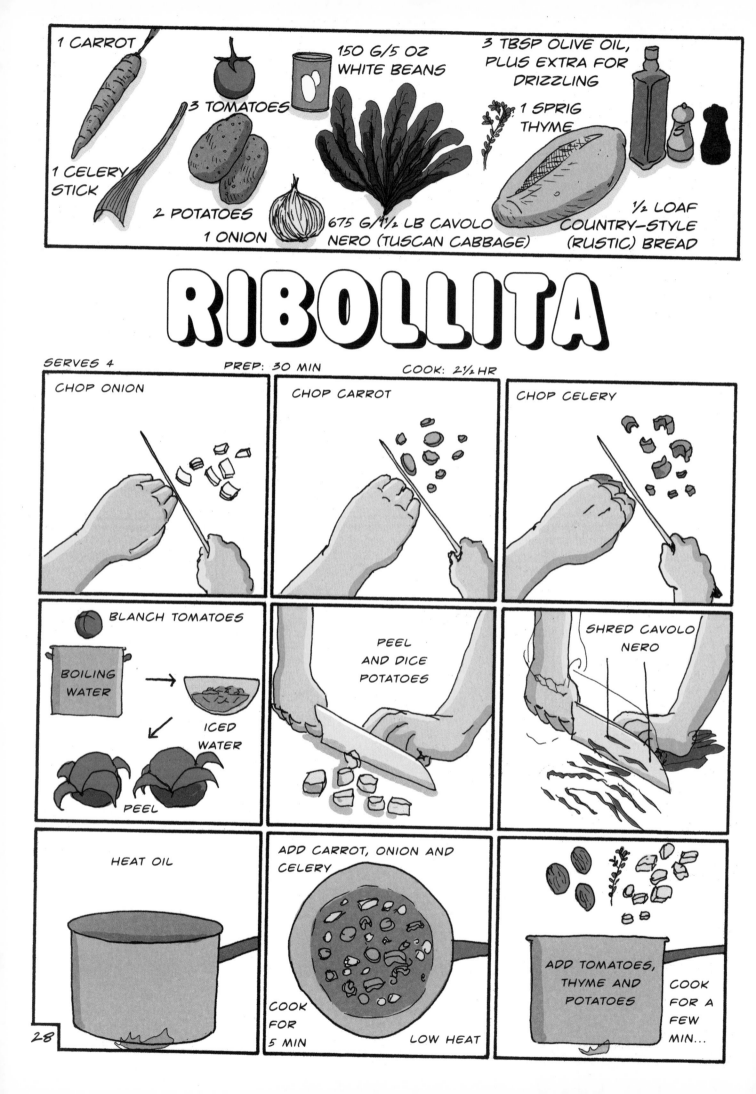

1 CARROT

3 TOMATOES

150 G/5 OZ WHITE BEANS

3 TBSP OLIVE OIL, PLUS EXTRA FOR DRIZZLING

1 CELERY STICK

2 POTATOES

1 ONION

675 G/1½ LB CAVOLO NERO (TUSCAN CABBAGE)

1 SPRIG THYME

½ LOAF COUNTRY-STYLE (RUSTIC) BREAD

RIBOLLITA

SERVES 4   PREP: 30 MIN   COOK: 2½ HR

CHOP ONION

CHOP CARROT

CHOP CELERY

BLANCH TOMATOES

BOILING WATER

ICED WATER

PEEL

PEEL AND DICE POTATOES

SHRED CAVOLO NERO

HEAT OIL

ADD CARROT, ONION AND CELERY

COOK FOR 5 MIN   LOW HEAT

ADD TOMATOES, THYME AND POTATOES

COOK FOR A FEW MIN...

PANZANELLA

8 SLICES RUSTIC (COUNTRY-STYLE) WHITE BREAD

8 BASIL LEAVES

EXTRA-VIRGIN OLIVE OIL, FOR DRIZZLING

4 FIRM RED TOMATOES

SERVES 4   PREP: 10 MIN

BLANCH TOMATOES

BOILING WATER

ICED WATER

PEEL   CHOP

REMOVE BREAD CRUSTS AND SOAK THE BREAD IN A BOWL OF COLD WATER FOR A FEW MIN

SQUEEZE OUT BREAD

AND PLACE IN A LARGE SALAD BOWL

SEASON THE BREAD

SPRINKLE WITH BASIL

DRIZZLE GENEROUSLY WITH OIL

RIP THE BREAD WITH TWO FORKS TO BREAK IT UP

ADD THE TOMATOES...

...AND SERVE

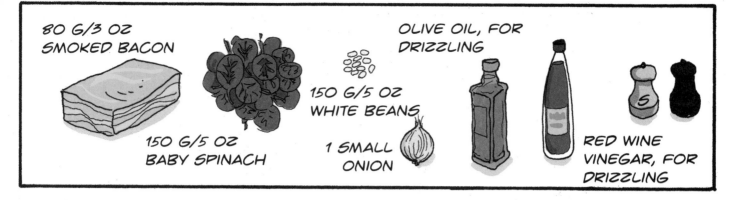

SPINACH SALAD WITH BACON & BEANS

SERVES 4   PREP: 10 MIN   COOK: 5 MIN

SOAK BEANS OVERNIGHT

Boil

UNTIL TENDER AND THEN DRAIN

GRILL

PREHEAT THE GRILL

LINE BAKING SHEET

WITH WAX PAPER

CHOP BACON   SLICE ONION

SPRINKLE BACON

ONTO LINED SHEET

GRILL BACON FOR 5 MIN UNTIL CRISP

ADD OIL AND VINEGAR + SEASON

GENTLY TOSS THE SALAD

BUON APPETITO

SPRINKLE THE SALAD WITH BACON

Ingredients

200 G/7 OZ RED OR YELLOW PEPPERS

200 G/7 OZ AUBERGINES

1 SPRIG PARSLEY

6 EGGS

25 G/1 OZ BUTTER

1 TBSP GRATED PARMESAN

100 G/3½ OZ FONTINA

OLIVE OIL

FRITTATA CAKE

SERVES 6   PREP: 30 MIN   COOK: 30 MIN

GRILL

PREHEAT GRILL

SLICE THE AUBERGINES AND GRILL UNTIL GOLDEN

CHOP PARSLEY

GRILL PEPPERS UNTIL BLACKENED AND CHARRED

TRANSFER TO A PLASTIC FOOD BAG AND SEAL THE TOP

PEEL

DE-SEED

CUT INTO STRIPS

PREHEAT OVEN TO 240°C/GAS MARK 9

2 EGGS

2 EGGS

IN SEPARATE BOWLS BEAT

BOWL 1

BOWL 2

DIVIDE PARSLEY BETWEEN THE 2 BOWLS AND SEASON

BOWL 1

BOWL 2

BEAT 2 EGGS AND PARMESAN AND SEASON

BOWL 3

HEAT 1 TBSP OLIVE OIL + THE BUTTER

POUR IN CONTENTS OF BOWL 1, COOK UNTIL SET ON ONE SIDE BUT STILL SOFT ON THE OTHER

THEN SLIDE THE FRITTATA ONTO A PLATE

COOK

THE CONTENTS OF THE OTHER 2 BOWLS IN THE SAME WAY

LINE A CAKE TIN WITH PARCHMENT PAPER

SLICE THE FONTINA

PLACE ONE PARSLEY FRITTATA IN THE TIN

SOFT SIDE UP

COVER WITH THE AUBERGINE AND HALF THE FONTINA

PLACE PARMESAN FRITTATA ON TOP, SOFT SIDE UP

TOP WITH PEPPER STRIPS AND REMAINING FONTINA

TOP WITH SECOND PARSLEY FRITTATA

SOFT SIDE DOWN

BAKE

FOR 10 MIN

SERVE HOT OR COLD

33

37

TAGLIATELLE WITH PEAS & HAM

SERVES 4   PREP: 15 MIN   COOK: 35 MIN

DICE HAM

THINLY SLICE ONION

COOK ONIONS UNTIL SOFT

LOW HEAT

THEN ADD PEAS

GRATE PARMESAN

AFTER 20 MIN STIR IN THE CREAM

AFTER 5 MIN ADD THE HAM

COOK TAGLIATELLE THEN DRAIN

TOSS

WITH THE PARMESAN

ECCO!

675 G/1½ LB SPINACH

2 EGG YOLKS

200 G/7 OZ PLAIN FLOUR

50 G/2 OZ PARMESAN

800 G/1¾ LB POTATOES

50 G/2 OZ BUTTER, MELTED

POTATO & SPINACH GNOCCHI

SERVES 4   PREP: 40 MIN   COOK: 25–30 MIN

Peel BOIL MASH

WASH, DRAIN AND COOK FOR 3–5 MIN

SQUEEZE SPINACH

THEN CHOP

MASH

MIX

SEASON

ADD EGG YOLKS

TO POTATO AND SPINACH

Knead

DON'T KNEAD TOO MUCH

SHAPE INTO A LONG ROLL

CUT INTO PIECES THEN PRESS AGAINST A GRATER...

2 CM/ ¾ INCH THICK

DUST WITH FLOUR

BOIL THEN REMOVE GNOCCHI WHEN THEY RISE TO SURFACE

SALTED BOILING WATER

MIX IN MELTED BUTTER AND GRATED PARMESAN

AND SERVE

...TO MAKE A PATTERN

1 SPRIG PARSLEY

800 G/1¾ LB CHANTERELLE MUSHROOMS

1 ONION

250 G/9 OZ CANNED TOMATOES

25 G/1 OZ BUTTER

25 G/1 OZ PARMESAN

350 G/12 OZ FUSILLI

3 TBSP OLIVE OIL

FUSILLI WITH MUSHROOMS

SERVES 4   PREP: 20 MIN   COOK: 1 HR

CHOP ONION

CHOP MUSHROOMS
1.
2.
3.

HEAT OIL

ADD TOMATOES AND SEASON

SIMMER FOR 45 MIN, REMOVE FROM HEAT AND ADD PARSLEY

BOIL FUSILLI

THEN DRAIN

SALTED BOILING WATER

ADD PARMESAN AND BUTTER TO FUSILLI AND TOSS

AND SERVE

SPAGHETTI CARBONARA

SERVES 4   PREP: 15 MIN   COOK: 20 MIN

GRATE BOTH CHEESES

DICE PANCETTA

ADD PANCETTA AND GARLIC CLOVE

MELT BUTTER... REMOVE CLOVE... ...WHEN GOLDEN

MEANWHILE... COOK THE PASTA

SALTED BOILING WATER

al dente.

LIGHTLY BEAT THE EGGS

DRAIN PASTA

RESERVE SOME COOKING WATER

ADD PASTA TO PANCETTA AND BUTTER

ADD A LITTLE COOKING WATER

ADD EGG AND SEASON

ADD HALF THE CHEESE AND...

TOSS

UNTIL THE EGG COATS THE PASTA

SPRINKLE WITH REMAINING CHEESE

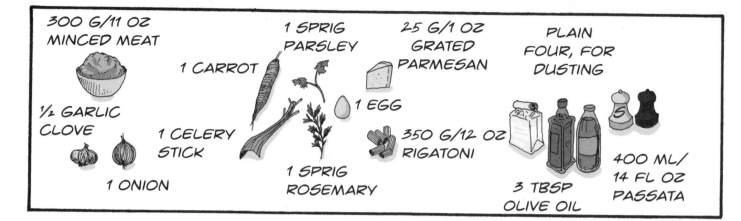

300 G/11 OZ MINCED MEAT

½ GARLIC CLOVE

1 ONION

1 CELERY STICK

1 CARROT

1 SPRIG PARSLEY

1 SPRIG ROSEMARY

1 EGG

25 G/1 OZ GRATED PARMESAN

350 G/12 OZ RIGATONI

3 TBSP OLIVE OIL

PLAIN FOUR, FOR DUSTING

400 ML/ 14 FL OZ PASSATA

RIGATONI WITH MEATBALLS

SERVES 4   PREP: 20 MIN   COOK: 1 HR

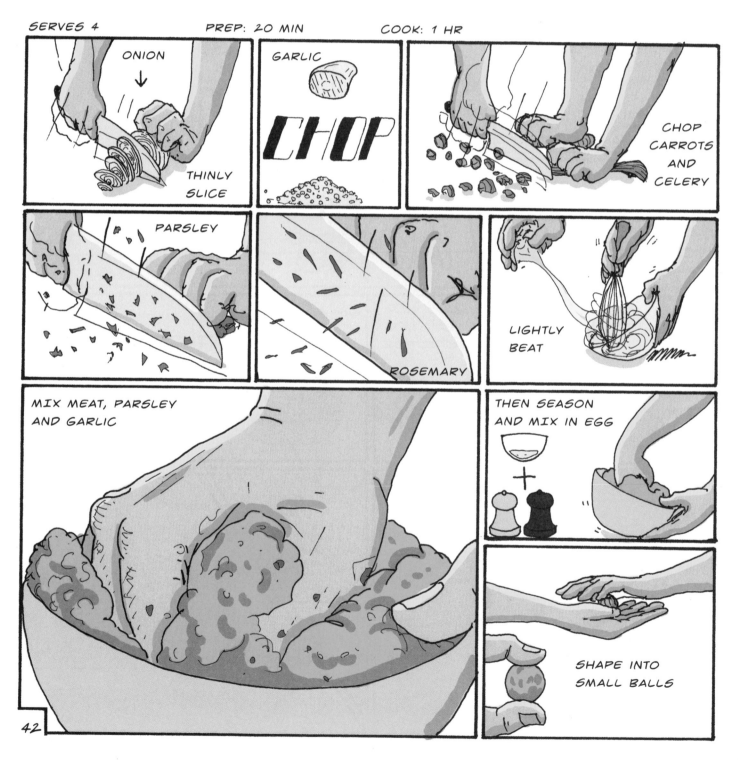

ONION — THINLY SLICE

GARLIC — CHOP

CHOP CARROTS AND CELERY

PARSLEY

ROSEMARY

LIGHTLY BEAT

MIX MEAT, PARSLEY AND GARLIC

THEN SEASON AND MIX IN EGG

SHAPE INTO SMALL BALLS

DUST WITH FLOUR

HEAT
OLIVE OIL
LOW HEAT

ONION CARROT CELERY ROSEMARY
COOK FOR 5 MIN
LOW HEAT

ADD MEATBALLS
MEDIUM HEAT

COOK UNTIL LIGHTLY BROWNED ALL OVER

SEASON AND ADD PASSATA

SIMMER FOR 40 MIN
STIRRING OCCASIONALLY

SALTED BOILING WATER

DRAIN

ADD TO PAN AND COOK FOR 2 MIN

DELIZIOSO!

TOP WITH PARMESAN

43

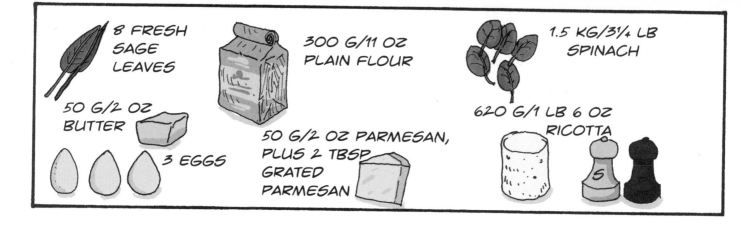

8 FRESH SAGE LEAVES

300 G/11 OZ PLAIN FLOUR

1.5 KG/3¼ LB SPINACH

50 G/2 OZ BUTTER

3 EGGS

50 G/2 OZ PARMESAN, PLUS 2 TBSP GRATED PARMESAN

620 G/1 LB 6 OZ RICOTTA

VEGETABLE- & CHEESE-FILLED RAVIOLI

SERVES 6   PREP: 2 HR   COOK: 10 MIN

PASTA

SIFT FLOUR AND PINCH SALT

MAKE A WELL

BEAT 2 EGGS AND 1 YOLK

POUR EGGS IN THE WELL

KNEAD

INCORPORATE EGGS INTO FLOUR

UNTIL SMOOTH THEN REST FOR 1 HR

FILLING

WASH, DRAIN AND COOK SPINACH FOR 5 MIN

CHOP SPINACH

MIX THE SPINACH WITH...

...500 G/1 LB 2 OZ RICOTTA

44

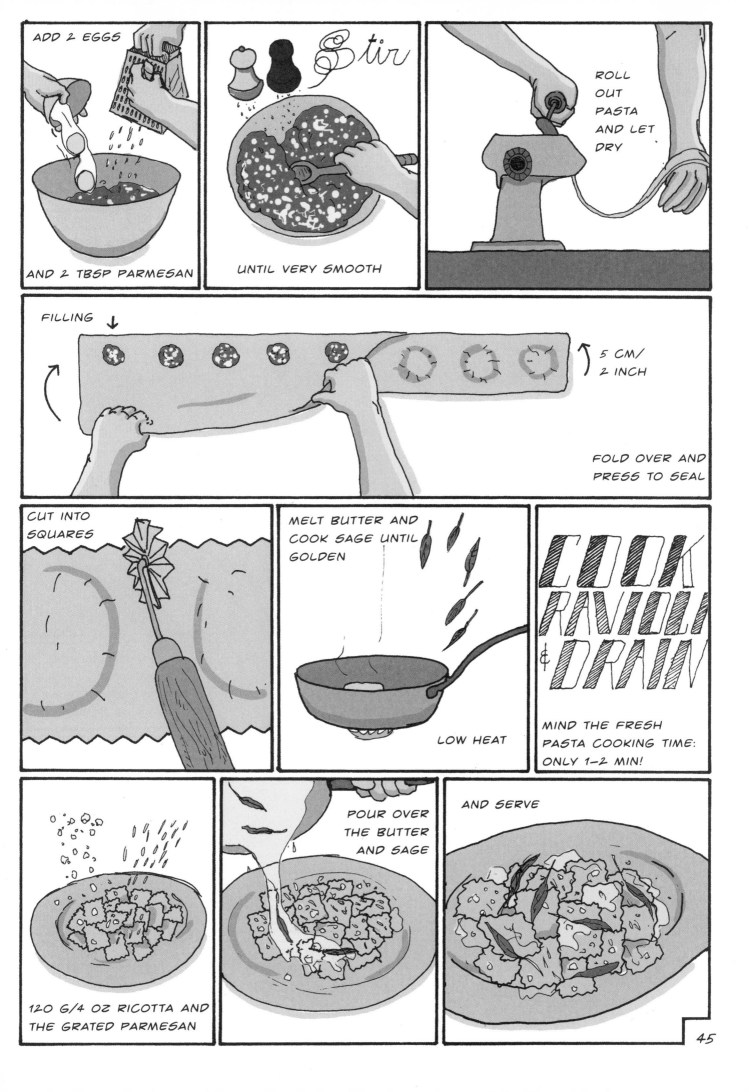

ADD 2 EGGS

AND 2 TBSP PARMESAN

Stir

UNTIL VERY SMOOTH

ROLL OUT PASTA AND LET DRY

FILLING ↓

5 CM/ 2 INCH

FOLD OVER AND PRESS TO SEAL

CUT INTO SQUARES

MELT BUTTER AND COOK SAGE UNTIL GOLDEN

LOW HEAT

COOK RAVIOLI & DRAIN

MIND THE FRESH PASTA COOKING TIME: ONLY 1–2 MIN!

120 G/4 OZ RICOTTA AND THE GRATED PARMESAN

POUR OVER THE BUTTER AND SAGE

AND SERVE

LINGUINE WITH PESTO

SERVES 4   PREP: 30 MIN   COOK: 12–15 MIN

GRATE PECORINO AND PARMESAN

GARLIC
SPINACH
CHOP
OIL AND SEASON
BLITZ IN A FOOD PROCESSOR UNTIL SMOOTH

ADD CHEESES

PEEL AND CUT POTATOES INTO BATONS

BOIL POTATO BATONS AND LINGUINE FOR 10 MIN THEN ADD THE BEANS...

SALTED BOILING WATER

...AND BOIL FOR ANOTHER 5 MIN OR UNTIL PASTA IS AL DENTE

DRAIN

TOSS WITH PESTO

AND SERVE

ALTERNATIVELY USE A PESTLE & MORTAR

GRIND UNTIL SMOOTH

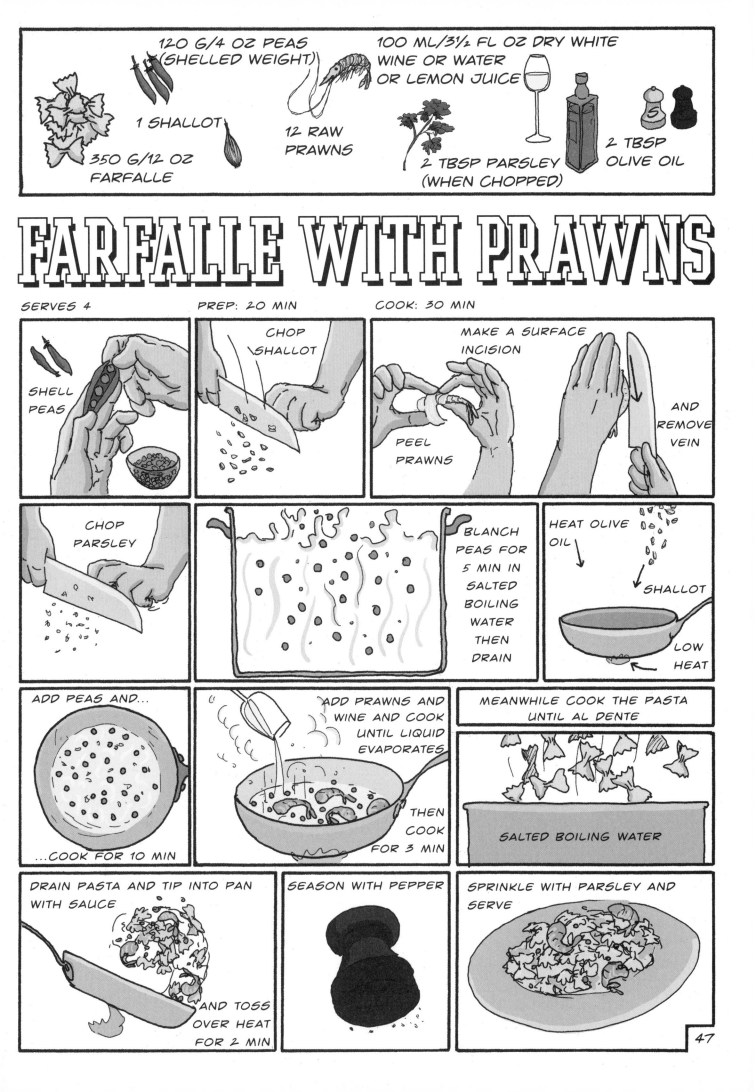

FARFALLE WITH PRAWNS

Ingredients:
- 120 G/4 OZ PEAS (SHELLED WEIGHT)
- 1 SHALLOT
- 350 G/12 OZ FARFALLE
- 12 RAW PRAWNS
- 100 ML/3½ FL OZ DRY WHITE WINE OR WATER OR LEMON JUICE
- 2 TBSP PARSLEY (WHEN CHOPPED)
- 2 TBSP OLIVE OIL

SERVES 4   PREP: 20 MIN   COOK: 30 MIN

SHELL PEAS

CHOP SHALLOT

MAKE A SURFACE INCISION

PEEL PRAWNS

AND REMOVE VEIN

CHOP PARSLEY

BLANCH PEAS FOR 5 MIN IN SALTED BOILING WATER THEN DRAIN

HEAT OLIVE OIL

SHALLOT

LOW HEAT

ADD PEAS AND...

...COOK FOR 10 MIN

ADD PRAWNS AND WINE AND COOK UNTIL LIQUID EVAPORATES

THEN COOK FOR 3 MIN

MEANWHILE COOK THE PASTA UNTIL AL DENTE

SALTED BOILING WATER

DRAIN PASTA AND TIP INTO PAN WITH SAUCE

AND TOSS OVER HEAT FOR 2 MIN

SEASON WITH PEPPER

SPRINKLE WITH PARSLEY AND SERVE

47

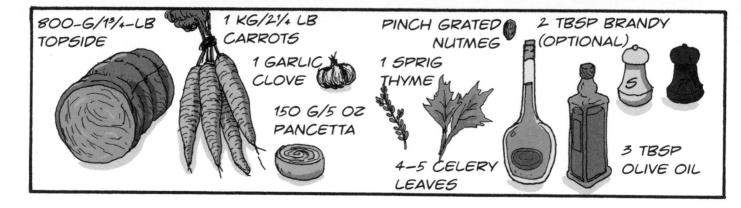

800-G/1¾-LB TOPSIDE

1 KG/2¼ LB CARROTS

1 GARLIC CLOVE

150 G/5 OZ PANCETTA

PINCH GRATED NUTMEG

1 SPRIG THYME

4-5 CELERY LEAVES

2 TBSP BRANDY (OPTIONAL)

3 TBSP OLIVE OIL

ROAST BEEF WITH CARROTS

SERVES 6   PREP: 20 MIN   COOK: 2½ HR

PREHEAT OVEN TO 125°C/ GAS MARK 1/2

SLICE THE CARROTS

THYME + GARLIC

CHOP CHOP CHOP

CHOP PANCETTA

SPRINKLE TWO-THIRDS INTO A ROASTING TRAY

HEAT THE OIL THEN COOK CARROTS, GARLIC AND THYME

MEDIUM HEAT

SEASON AND ADD NUTMEG

KEEP WARM

TIE THE MEAT WITH STRING

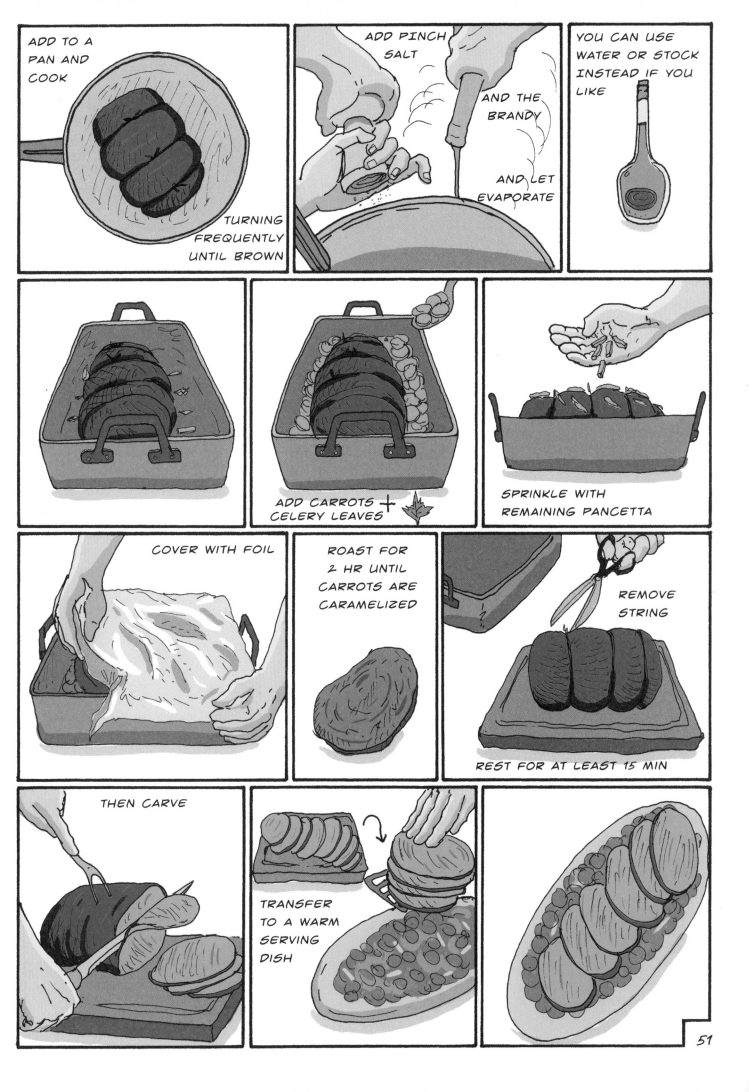

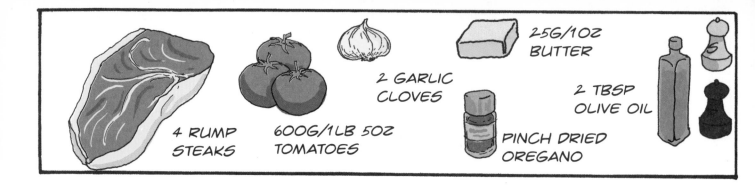

STEAK PIZZAIOLA

SERVES 4   PREP: 30 MIN   COOK: 10 MIN

BLANCH TOMATOES

BOILING WATER → ICED WATER

PEEL → ↓CHOP

WHEN HOT ADD GARLIC, FRY UNTIL BROWN, THEN REMOVE AND DISCARD

COOK 1 MINUTE EACH SIDE

KEEP WARM

TOMATO   OREGANO

COOK UNTIL THICKENED AND PULPY

RETURN TO THE PAN

AND COOK TO YOUR LIKING

RARE   MEDIUM   WELL-DONE

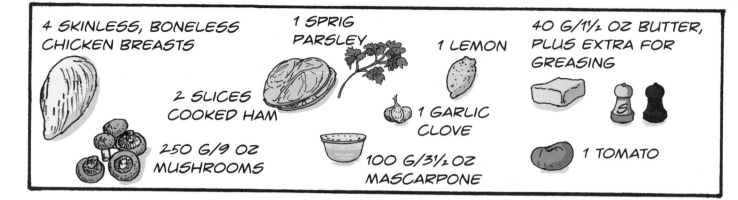

4 SKINLESS, BONELESS CHICKEN BREASTS

2 SLICES COOKED HAM

250 G/9 OZ MUSHROOMS

1 SPRIG PARSLEY

1 LEMON

1 GARLIC CLOVE

100 G/3½ OZ MASCARPONE

40 G/1½ OZ BUTTER, PLUS EXTRA FOR GREASING

1 TOMATO

CHICKEN STUFFED WITH MASCARPONE

SERVES 4   PREP: 50 MIN   COOK: 30 MIN

PREHEAT OVEN TO 200°C/ GAS MARK 6

GREASE A ROASTING TIN WITH BUTTER

CHOP MUSHROOMS

SQUEEZE LEMON

CHOP PARSLEY

MELT 25 G/1 OZ BUTTER

LOW HEAT

ADD GARLIC AND REMOVE AND DISCARD WHEN BROWN

MUSHROOMS

PARSLEY

HIGH HEAT

COOK FOR 5 MIN THEN...

...REMOVE FROM HEAT AND SEASON

CAREFULLY SLICE ALMOST ALL THE WAY THROUGH THE BREASTS

54

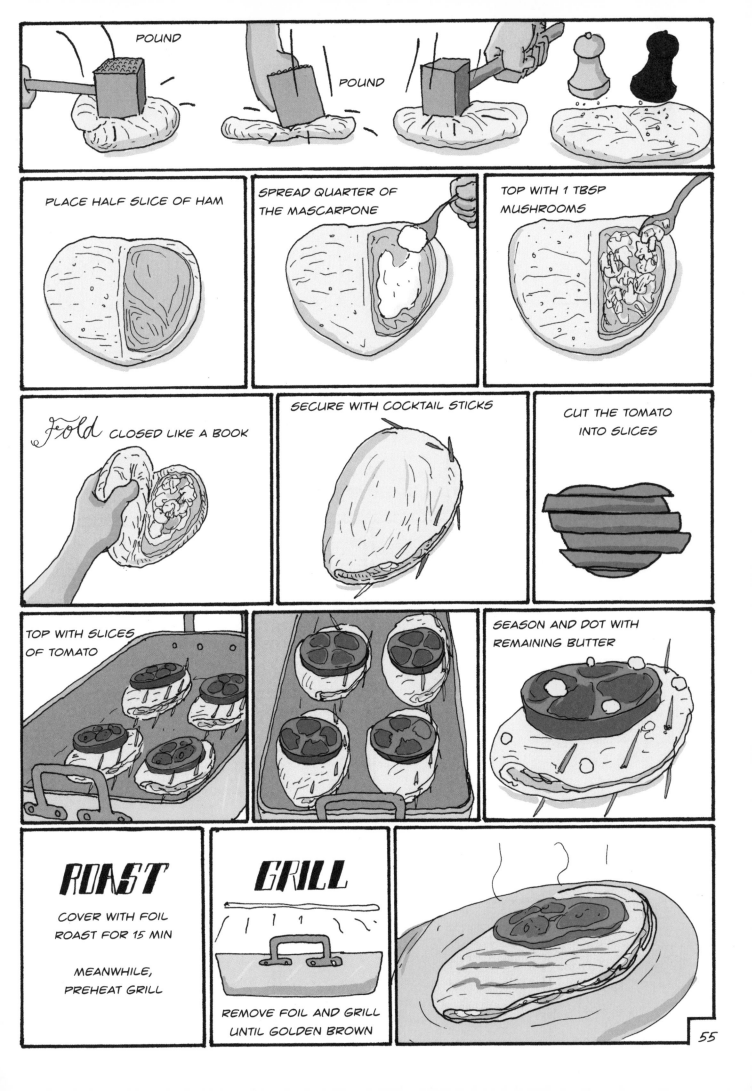

POUND

POUND

PLACE HALF SLICE OF HAM

SPREAD QUARTER OF THE MASCARPONE

TOP WITH 1 TBSP MUSHROOMS

Fold CLOSED LIKE A BOOK

SECURE WITH COCKTAIL STICKS

CUT THE TOMATO INTO SLICES

TOP WITH SLICES OF TOMATO

SEASON AND DOT WITH REMAINING BUTTER

ROAST

COVER WITH FOIL ROAST FOR 15 MIN

MEANWHILE, PREHEAT GRILL

GRILL

REMOVE FOIL AND GRILL UNTIL GOLDEN BROWN

40 G/1½ OZ BUTTER

4 PORK LOIN CHOPS, TRIMMED OF BONES

6 SAGE LEAVES

PORK CHOPS WITH BUTTER & SAGE

SERVES 4   PREP: 10 MIN   COOK: 15 MIN

BASH

WITH A MEAT MALLET

MELT THE BUTTER AND THEN ADD THE SAGE

LOW HEAT

DON'T BURN

THE BUTTER...

...OR THE SAGE

ADD THE MEAT AND COOK FOR ABOUT 5 MIN EACH SIDE...

...UNTIL TENDER AND COOKED THROUGH THEN SEASON

SERVE WITH ROAST OR MASHED POTATOES

AND SAVOY CABBAGE, BROCCOLI OR FRENCH BEANS

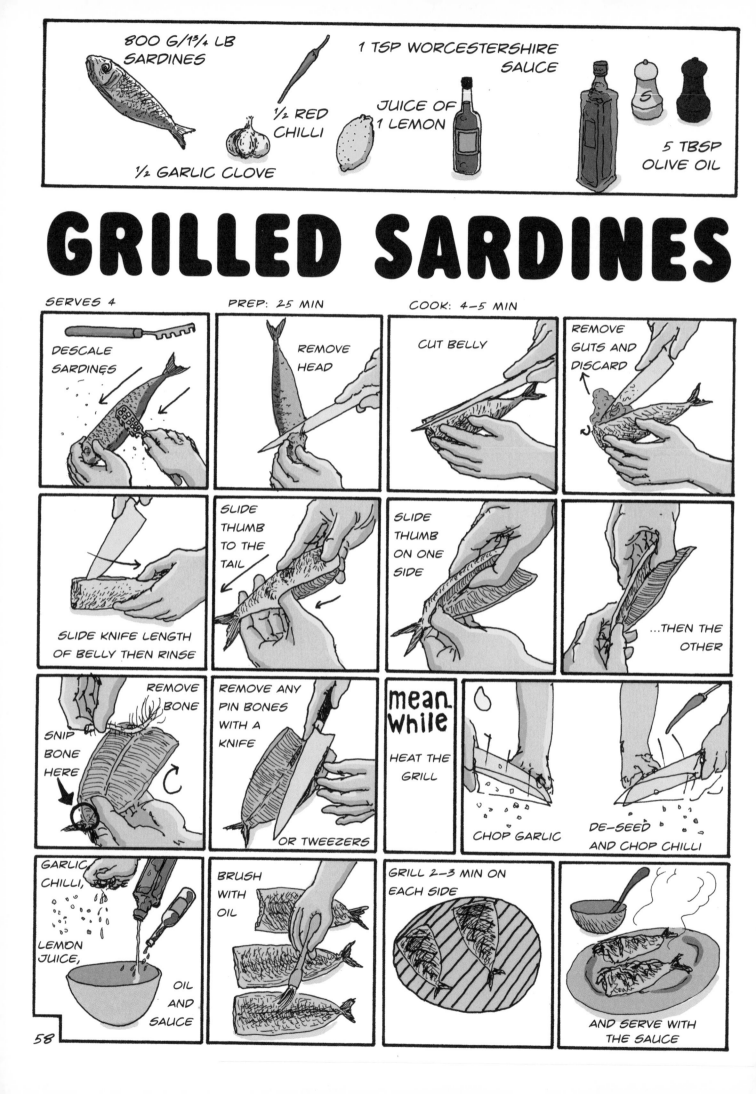

GRILLED SARDINES

HAKE IN GREEN SAUCE

1 ONION

1 CELERY STALK, PLUS A FEW LEAVES

4 HAKE STEAKS

1 SPRIG PARSLEY

JUICE OF 1 LEMON

2 TBSP OLIVE OIL, PLUS EXTRA FOR BRUSHING

SERVES 4   PREP: 15 MIN   COOK: 10 MIN

PREHEAT OVEN TO 200°C/GAS MARK 6

ONION

CELERY

PARSLEY

CHOP CHOP CHOP

CHOP CHOP CHOP

BRUSH OVENPROOF DISH WITH OIL

COOK STEAKS FOR 10 MIN MEANWHILE, MAKE THE SAUCE...

HEAT 2 TBSP OLIVE OIL

COOK ONION FOR 5 MIN UNTIL SOFT

LOW HEAT

SEASON

THEN REMOVE FROM THE HEAT

PARSLEY

CELERY

LEMON JUICE

POUR SAUCE OVER HAKE AND SERVE

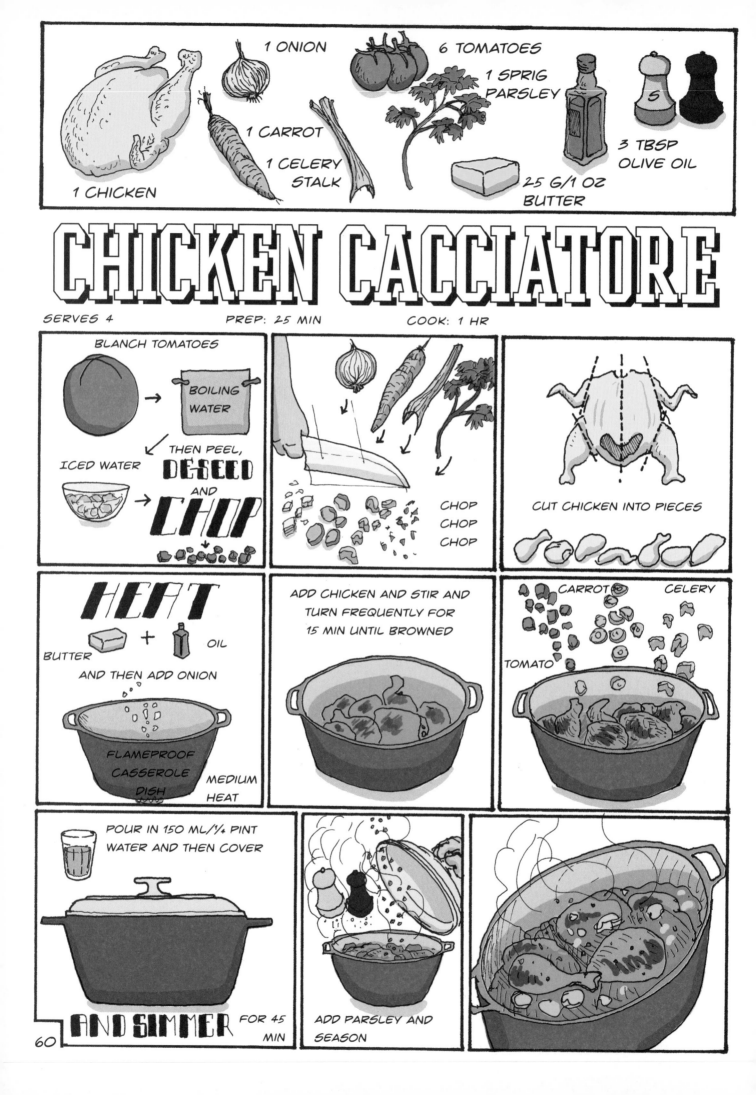

1 ONION

6 TOMATOES

1 SPRIG PARSLEY

3 TBSP OLIVE OIL

1 CARROT

1 CELERY STALK

25 G/1 OZ BUTTER

1 CHICKEN

CHICKEN CACCIATORE

SERVES 4   PREP: 25 MIN   COOK: 1 HR

BLANCH TOMATOES

BOILING WATER

ICED WATER

THEN PEEL, DESEED AND CHOP

CHOP CHOP CHOP

CUT CHICKEN INTO PIECES

HEAT

BUTTER + OIL

AND THEN ADD ONION

FLAMEPROOF CASSEROLE DISH   MEDIUM HEAT

ADD CHICKEN AND STIR AND TURN FREQUENTLY FOR 15 MIN UNTIL BROWNED

CARROT   CELERY

TOMATO

POUR IN 150 ML/¼ PINT WATER AND THEN COVER

AND SIMMER FOR 45 MIN

ADD PARSLEY AND SEASON

1 CHICKEN

1 KG/2¼ LB SEA SALT

1 EGG WHITE

1 SPRIG ROSEMARY

1 KG/2¼ LB PLAIN FLOUR

1 BAY LEAF

CHICKEN IN A SALT CRUST

SERVES 4   PREP: 30 MIN   COOK: 1½ HR

PREHEAT OVEN TO 160°C/GAS MARK 3

MIX SALT AND FLOUR THEN...

...ADD THE EGG WHITE AND MIX THOROUGHLY

ADD HERBS

SEASON

PLACE IN AN OVEN-PROOF DISH

COMPLETELY COVER WITH THE SALT MIXTURE

COVER TIGHTLY

BAKE FOR 1½ HR

REMOVE LID AND BREAK

SALT CRUST

CUT INTO PIECES

AND SERVE

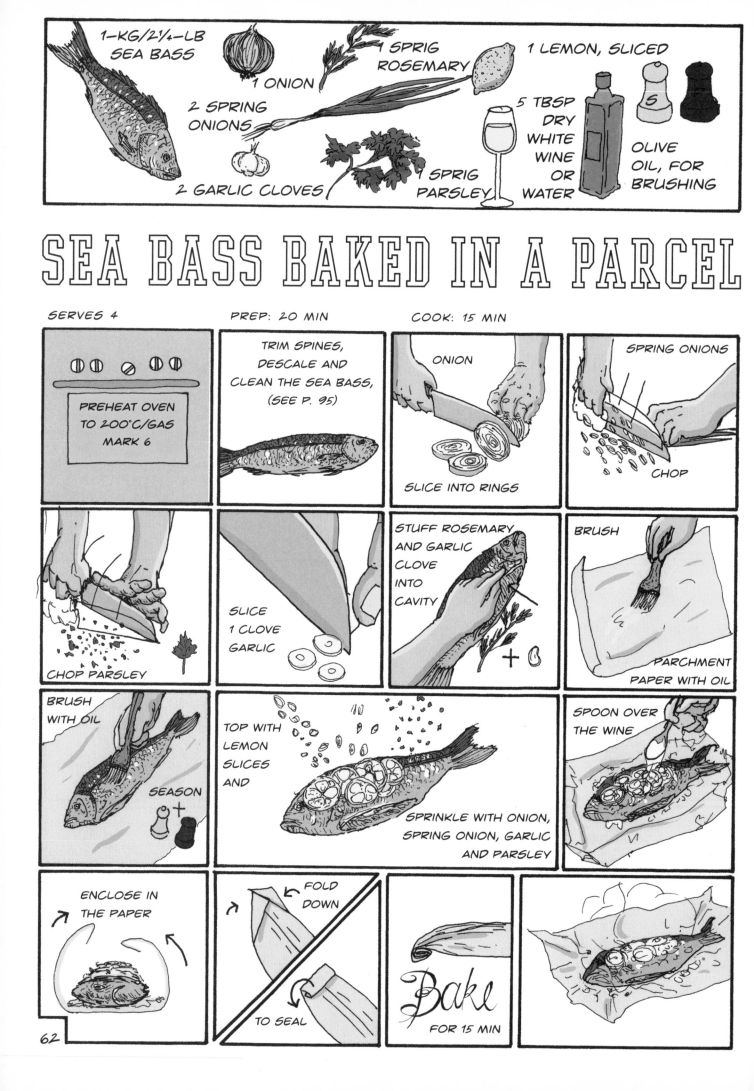

SEA BASS BAKED IN A PARCEL

Ingredients:
- 1-KG/2¼-LB SEA BASS
- 1 ONION
- 2 SPRING ONIONS
- 2 GARLIC CLOVES
- 1 SPRIG ROSEMARY
- 1 SPRIG PARSLEY
- 1 LEMON, SLICED
- 5 TBSP DRY WHITE WINE OR WATER
- S
- OLIVE OIL, FOR BRUSHING

SERVES 4   PREP: 20 MIN   COOK: 15 MIN

PREHEAT OVEN TO 200°C/GAS MARK 6

TRIM SPINES, DESCALE AND CLEAN THE SEA BASS, (SEE P. 95)

ONION — SLICE INTO RINGS

SPRING ONIONS — CHOP

CHOP PARSLEY

SLICE 1 CLOVE GARLIC

STUFF ROSEMARY AND GARLIC CLOVE INTO CAVITY

BRUSH PARCHMENT PAPER WITH OIL

BRUSH WITH OIL — SEASON

TOP WITH LEMON SLICES AND SPRINKLE WITH ONION, SPRING ONION, GARLIC AND PARSLEY

SPOON OVER THE WINE

ENCLOSE IN THE PAPER

FOLD DOWN — TO SEAL

Bake FOR 15 MIN

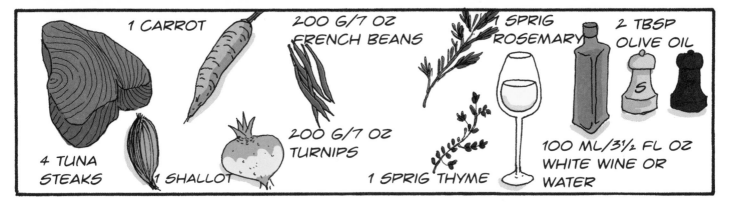

1 CARROT

200 G/7 OZ FRENCH BEANS

1 SPRIG ROSEMARY

2 TBSP OLIVE OIL

200 G/7 OZ TURNIPS

4 TUNA STEAKS

1 SHALLOT

1 SPRIG THYME

100 ML/3½ FL OZ WHITE WINE OR WATER

SLOW-COOKED TUNA

SERVES 4   PREP: 20 MIN   COOK: 55 MIN

CHOP

HALVE

HEAT OLIVE OIL THEN ADD TUNA AND COOK → UNTIL → BROWN ON BOTH SIDES

REMOVE TUNA

SKIM FAT

COOK SHALLOTS FOR ABOUT 5 MIN

THEN ADD CARROTS, TURNIPS, BEANS, THYME AND ROSEMARY

MEDIUM HEAT

SEASON AND COOK FOR ABOUT 40 MIN

RETURN TUNA TO PAN

POUR IN WINE AND

150 ML/ 5 FL OZ WARM WATER

COVER

AND SIMMER

FOR 30 MIN

DISCARD HERBS AND SERVE

ASPARAGUS RISOTTO

350 G/12 OZ RISOTTO RICE

½ ONION

2 POTATOES

2 TURNIPS

3 TBSP OLIVE OIL

2 CARROTS

65 G/2½ OZ BUTTER

2 ONIONS

1 CELERY STICK

PARMESAN, TO SERVE

2 LEEKS, TRIMMED

3 CHERRY TOMATOES

500 G/1 LB 2 OZ ASPARAGUS

SERVES 4   PREP: 1¼ HR   COOK: 30 MIN

STOCK

COARSELY CHOP

ADD PINCH SALT

POUR IN 1.5 LITRES/ 2½ PINTS WATER

BRING TO THE BOIL THEN REDUCE HEAT AND SIMMER FOR 20 MIN

REMOVE FROM HEAT, STRAIN AND KEEP LIQUID

CHOP ONION

TRIM ENDS OF ASPARAGUS

BOIL ASPARAGUS FOR 5 MIN OR UNTIL TENDER

SALTED BOILING WATER

DRAIN AND CUT OFF ASPARAGUS TIPS

SET TIPS ASIDE

CHOP STEMS AND SET ASIDE

BRING STOCK TO THE BOIL AND MELT 15 G/½ OZ BUTTER

HIGH HEAT   LOW HEAT

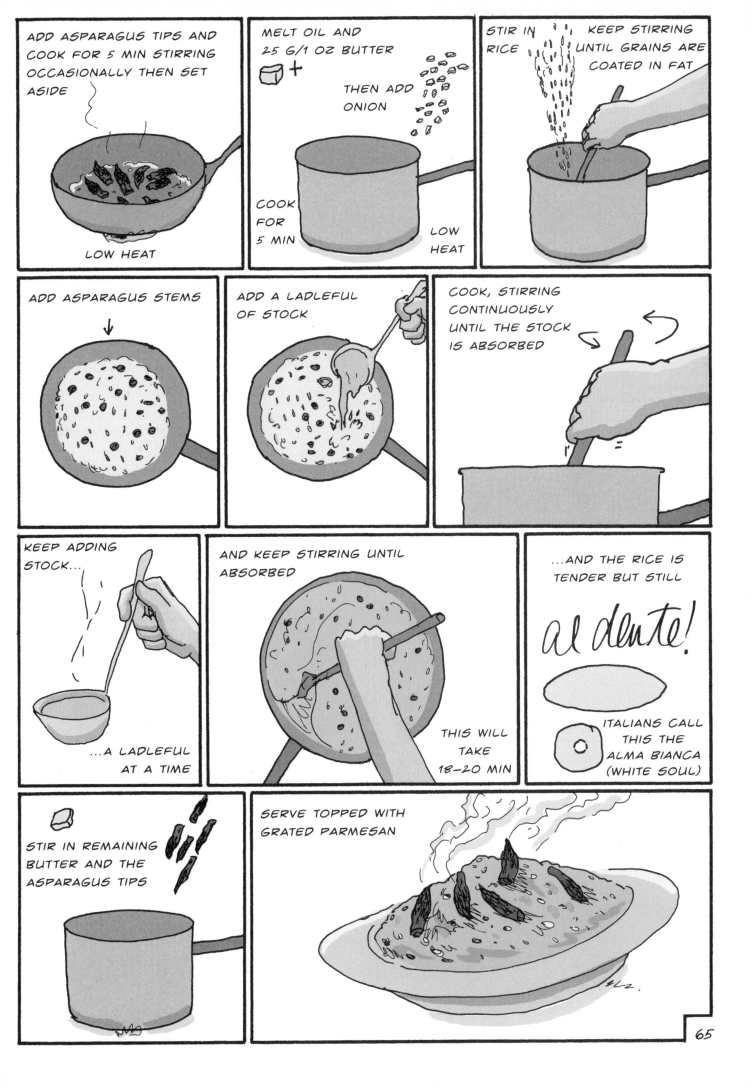

ADD ASPARAGUS TIPS AND COOK FOR 5 MIN STIRRING OCCASIONALLY THEN SET ASIDE

LOW HEAT

MELT OIL AND 25 G/1 OZ BUTTER + THEN ADD ONION

COOK FOR 5 MIN

LOW HEAT

STIR IN RICE   KEEP STIRRING UNTIL GRAINS ARE COATED IN FAT

ADD ASPARAGUS STEMS

ADD A LADLEFUL OF STOCK

COOK, STIRRING CONTINUOUSLY UNTIL THE STOCK IS ABSORBED

KEEP ADDING STOCK...

...A LADLEFUL AT A TIME

AND KEEP STIRRING UNTIL ABSORBED

THIS WILL TAKE 18-20 MIN

...AND THE RICE IS TENDER BUT STILL

al dente!

ITALIANS CALL THIS THE ALMA BIANCA (WHITE SOUL)

STIR IN REMAINING BUTTER AND THE ASPARAGUS TIPS

SERVE TOPPED WITH GRATED PARMESAN

1 KG/2¼ LB AUBERGINES

2 GARLIC CLOVES

2.5 KG/5½ LB MUSSELS

175 ML/6 FL OZ DRY WHITE WINE

1 KG/2¼ LB RAW PRAWNS

2.5 KG/5½ LB CLAMS

1 TBSP SAGE (WHEN FINELY CHOPPED

4 EGGS, SEPARATED

1 KG/2¼ LB SQUID, (SEE P. 95)

6 TBSP OLIVE OIL, PLUS EXTRA FOR DEEP-FRYING

500 G/1 LB 2 OZ PLAIN FLOUR, PLUS EXTRA FOR DUSTING

1 KG/2¼ LB COURGETTES

3 PEPPERS

FRITTO MISTO

SERVES 16   PREP: 1½ HR   COOK: 30–40 MIN

SLICE AUBERGINES

CUT PEPPERS INTO 3-CM SQUARES

SLICE COURGETTE

SCRUB AND CLEAN CLAMS AND MUSSELS DISCARDING ANY DAMAGED OR OPEN ONES (SEE P.95)

CUT SQUID INTO RINGS

HEAT 3 TBSP OIL + 1 GARLIC CLOVE

ADD MUSSELS, COVER AND COOK FOR 4–5 MIN UNTIL SHELLS OPEN

REMOVE MUSSELS WITH SLOTTED SPOON DISCARD ANY THAT REMAIN SHUT AND REMOVE REST FROM THEIR SHELLS

HEAT 3 TBSP OIL + 1 GARLIC CLOVE IN ANOTHER LARGE PAN

ADD CLAMS COVER AND COOK FOR 3–5 MIN UNTIL SHELLS OPEN

DISCARD ANY CLAMS THAT REMAIN SHUT REMOVE REST FROM THEIR SHELLS

COOK FOR 2 MIN SALTED BOILING WATER

66

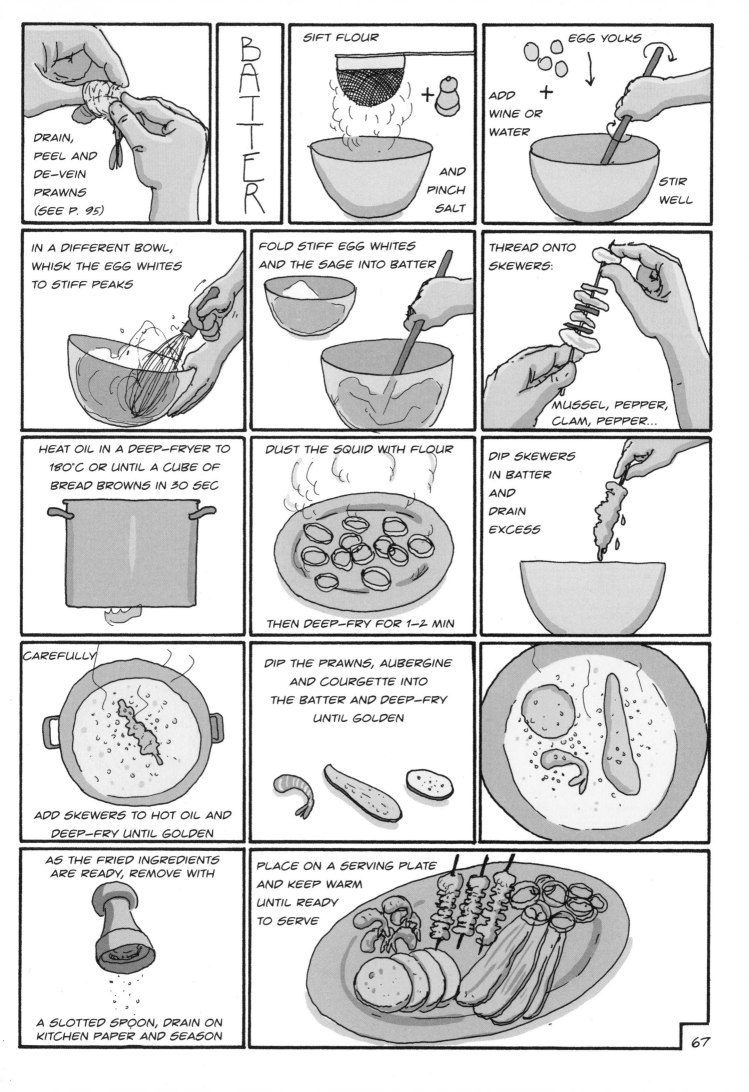

ROCKET & TALEGGIO PIE

SERVES 6   PREP: 15 MIN, PLUS 1 HR RESTING   COOK: 40 MIN

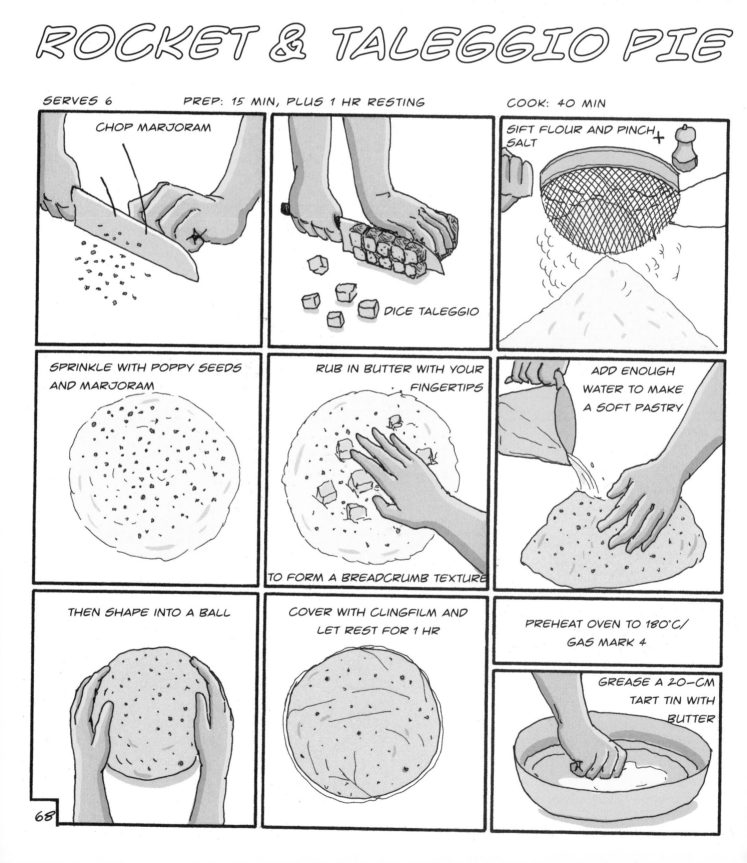

CHOP MARJORAM

DICE TALEGGIO

SIFT FLOUR AND PINCH SALT

SPRINKLE WITH POPPY SEEDS AND MARJORAM

RUB IN BUTTER WITH YOUR FINGERTIPS

TO FORM A BREADCRUMB TEXTURE

ADD ENOUGH WATER TO MAKE A SOFT PASTRY

THEN SHAPE INTO A BALL

COVER WITH CLINGFILM AND LET REST FOR 1 HR

PREHEAT OVEN TO 180°C/ GAS MARK 4

GREASE A 20–CM TART TIN WITH BUTTER

BLANCH ROCKET FOR 1 MIN

SALTED BOILING WATER

THEN DRAIN, LET COOL AND SQUEEZE OUT LIQUID

BLITZ ROCKET, BOTH CHEESES, BREAD-CRUMBS AND EGGS IN A PROCESSOR AND SEASON

ROLL OUT PASTRY...

...AND USE IT TO LINE THE PREPARED TIN

TRIM EDGES OF PASTRY AND RESERVE TRIMMINGS

FILL WITH ROCKET AND CHEESE MIXTURE

ROLL OUT THE TRIMMINGS

CUT INTO THIN STRIPS AND BRUSH THE ENDS WITH WATER

ARRANGE STRIPS IN A LATTICE OVER THE TOP OF THE PIE

Bake

FOR 40 MIN

69

DESSERTS & BAKING

200 G/7 OZ PLAIN FLOUR

150 G/5 OZ UNSALTED BUTTER

4 PEARS

130 G/4½ OZ PLAIN CHOCOLATE, BROKEN INTO PIECES

100 ML/3½ FL OZ DOUBLE CREAM

80 G/3 OZ CASTER SUGAR

4 TBSP GRAND MARNIER OR ORANGE JUICE

25 G/1 OZ BLANCHED ALMONDS, CHOPPED

CHOCOLATE & PEAR TART

SERVES 8   PREP: 1 HR, PLUS 1 HR STANDING & COOLING   COOK: 25 MIN

SIFT FLOUR, 1 TBSP SUGAR AND PINCH SALT

100 G/3½ OZ BUTTER

USING A CRISS-CROSS MOTION WITH 2 KNIVES, CUT THE BUTTER INTO THE FLOUR UNTIL PIECES ARE TINY

RUB IN THE BUTTER WITH FINGER TIPS...

...UNTIL IT RESEMBLES FINE BREADCRUMBS

SPRINKLE 4-5 TBSP ICED WATER

STIR INTO MIXTURE TO FORM A DOUGH

SHAPE DOUGH INTO A FLAT DISC

COVER WITH CLINGFILM

LEAVE TO STAND FOR 1 HR

MEANWHILE...

PEEL THE PEARS

HALVE AND CORE

SPRINKLE WITH SUGAR AND GRAND MARNIER

PREHEAT OVEN TO 180°C/GAS MARK 4

ROLL OUT THE PASTRY UNTIL...

...4–5 MM THICK

LINE A 22.5-CM TART TIN WITH THE PASTRY AND THEN LINE WITH FOIL

FOIL

POUR IN BAKING BEANS

BAKE IN OVEN FOR 10 MIN

REMOVE FOIL AND BEANS

PLACE PEARS IN PASTRY CASE

RETURN TO OVEN AND BAKE UNTIL PASTRY CRUST IS GOLDEN BROWN

REMOVE FROM OVEN THEN LET COOL

MELT CHOCOLATE WITH 1 TBSP WATER

LOW HEAT

ADD REMAINING BUTTER, MELT, THEN REMOVE FROM HEAT AND LET COOL

WHIP CREAM

FOLD CREAM INTO CHOCOLATE

COVER PEARS

SPRINKLE WITH ALMONDS AND SERVE

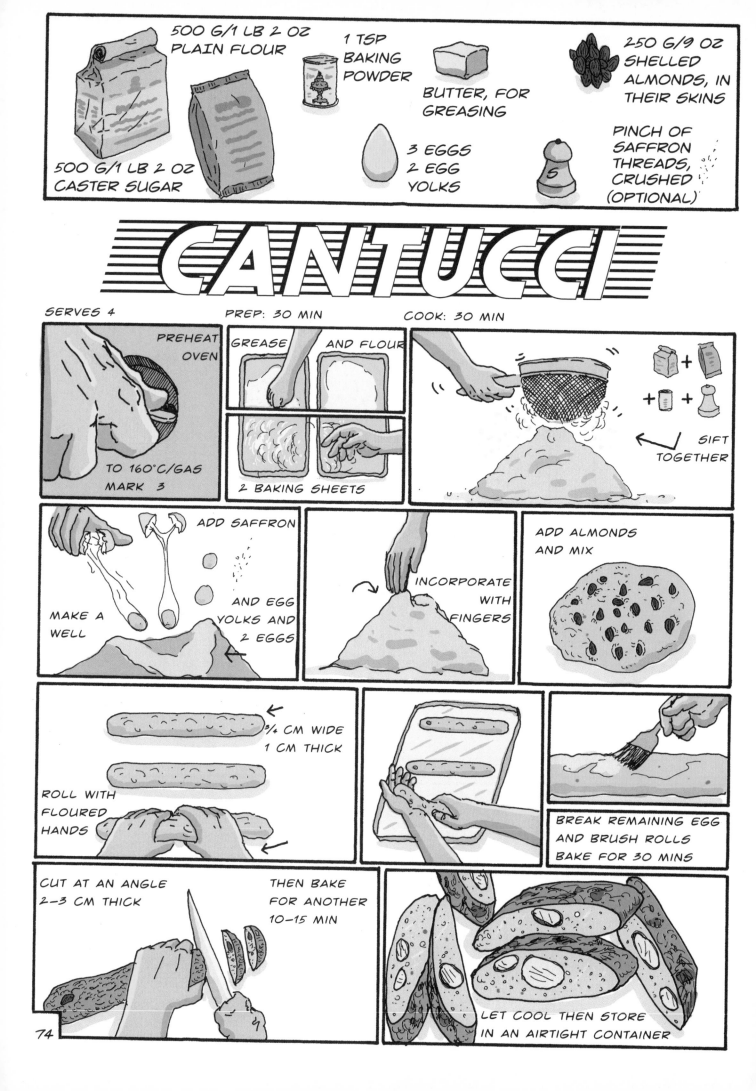

500 G/1 LB 2 OZ PLAIN FLOUR

1 TSP BAKING POWDER

BUTTER, FOR GREASING

250 G/9 OZ SHELLED ALMONDS, IN THEIR SKINS

500 G/1 LB 2 OZ CASTER SUGAR

3 EGGS
2 EGG YOLKS

PINCH OF SAFFRON THREADS, CRUSHED (OPTIONAL)

CANTUCCI

SERVES 4   PREP: 30 MIN   COOK: 30 MIN

PREHEAT OVEN TO 160°C/GAS MARK 3

GREASE AND FLOUR 2 BAKING SHEETS

SIFT TOGETHER

MAKE A WELL

ADD SAFFRON AND EGG YOLKS AND 2 EGGS

INCORPORATE WITH FINGERS

ADD ALMONDS AND MIX

ROLL WITH FLOURED HANDS

¾ CM WIDE
1 CM THICK

BREAK REMAINING EGG AND BRUSH ROLLS
BAKE FOR 30 MINS

CUT AT AN ANGLE 2-3 CM THICK

THEN BAKE FOR ANOTHER 10-15 MIN

LET COOL THEN STORE IN AN AIRTIGHT CONTAINER

250 G/9 OZ
RASPBERRIES

750 ML/1¼ PINTS
DOUBLE CREAM

6 EGGS

250 G/9 OZ
CASTER SUGAR

RASPBERRY SEMIFREDDO

SERVES 6–8   PREP: 30 MIN, PLUS 4 HR FREEZING   COOK: 10–15 MIN

LINE A 20-CM LOAF TIN WITH CLINGFILM

WHISK EGGS AND SUGAR IN HEATPROOF BOWL OVER PAN UNTIL THICK →

MUST NOT TOUCH WATER

BARELY SIMMERING WATER

REMOVE FROM HEAT

CONTINUE WHISKING UNTIL THICKENED

MASH RASPBERRIES

WHIP CREAM TO STIFF PEAKS

STIR EGG MIXTURE

AND RASPBERRIES INTO CREAM

POUR MIXTURE INTO TIN

FREEZE FOR AT LEAST 4 HR

SERVE IN SLICES

200 G/ 7 OZ SELF-RAISING FLOUR

80 G/3 OZ UNSALTED BUTTER, SOFTENED, PLUS EXTRA FOR GREASING

WHIPPED CREAM, TO SERVE (OPTIONAL)

150 G/5 OZ CASTER SUGAR

3 APPLES

3 EGGS, ROOM TEMPERATURE

APPLE CAKE

SERVES 6   PREP: 35 MIN, PLUS COOLING   COOK: 40 MIN

PREHEAT THE OVEN

TO 180°C/GAS MARK 4

GREASE A 20-CM CAKE TIN

PEEL AND CORE...

...THEN CHOP

3 EGGS + SUGAR

WHISK UNTIL PALE AND FLUFFY AND THICK ENOUGH TO LEAVE A RIBBON

...ABOUT 10–12 MIN

THEN BEAT IN 1 TBSP BUTTER

DON'T WORRY IF MIXTURE LOOKS LUMPY!

ADD FLOUR IN 2 PARTS ALTERNATING WITH THE APPLES

MIX GENTLY THEN TRANSFER TO THE TIN

Bake

FOR 40 MIN THEN LET COOL

TURN OUT

AND SERVE WITH WHIPPED CREAM IF YOU LIKE

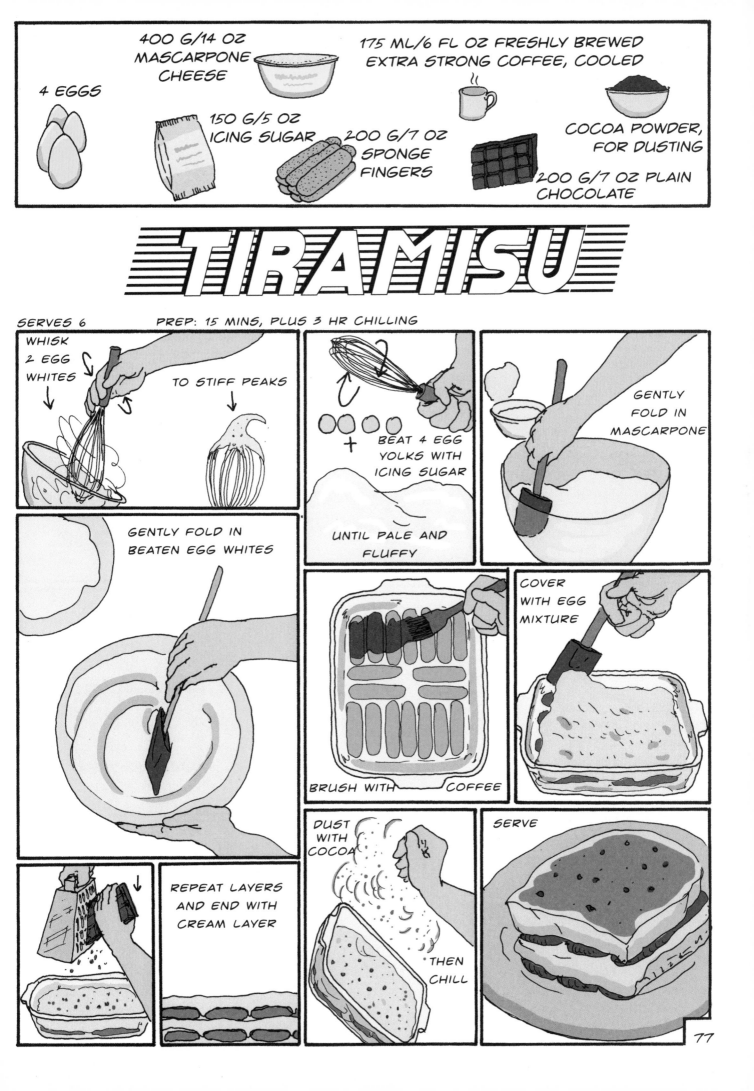

400 G/14 OZ MASCARPONE CHEESE

4 EGGS

150 G/5 OZ ICING SUGAR

200 G/7 OZ SPONGE FINGERS

175 ML/6 FL OZ FRESHLY BREWED EXTRA STRONG COFFEE, COOLED

COCOA POWDER, FOR DUSTING

200 G/7 OZ PLAIN CHOCOLATE

TIRAMISU

SERVES 6   PREP: 15 MINS, PLUS 3 HR CHILLING

WHISK 2 EGG WHITES

TO STIFF PEAKS

BEAT 4 EGG YOLKS WITH ICING SUGAR

UNTIL PALE AND FLUFFY

GENTLY FOLD IN MASCARPONE

GENTLY FOLD IN BEATEN EGG WHITES

BRUSH WITH   COFFEE

COVER WITH EGG MIXTURE

REPEAT LAYERS AND END WITH CREAM LAYER

DUST WITH COCOA

THEN CHILL

SERVE

10 G/¼ OZ GELATINE LEAVES

100 G/3½ OZ CASTER SUGAR

25 G/1 OZ PLAIN FLOUR

4 EGG YOLKS

A FEW DROPS VANILLA ESSENCE

OR 1 TSP LEMON ZEST

475 ML/16 FL OZ DOUBLE CREAM

1 VANILLA POD, SLIT

VEGETABLE OIL, FOR BRUSHING

100 ML/ 3½ FL OZ MILK

100 G/3½ OZ CASTER SUGAR

100 G/3½ OZ HAZELNUTS, SHELLED

500 ML/18 FL OZ MILK

PANNA COTTA

SERVES 6   PREP: 35 MIN, PLUS COOLING   COOK: 40 MIN

SOAK GELATINE LEAVES IN WATER FOR 3–5 MIN

HEAT 100 ML/3½ MILK TO JUST BELOW SIMMERING POINT

↓

TAKE CARE NOT TO LET IT BOIL

← LOW HEAT

THEN REMOVE MILK FROM HEAT

DRAIN GELATINE LEAVES AND ADD TO MILK

POUR CREAM INTO A SEPARATE PAN

ADD VANILLA AND 100 G/ 3½ OZ SUGAR TO CREAM

AND BOIL OVER LOW HEAT, STIRRING CONTINUOUSLY

REMOVE FROM HEAT AND REMOVE VANILLA POD

STIR MILK AND GELATINE MIXTURE INTO VANILLA CREAM MIXTURE

BRUSH MOULDS WITH OIL

POUR IN MIXTURE

AND CHILL FOR AT LEAST 4 HR

78

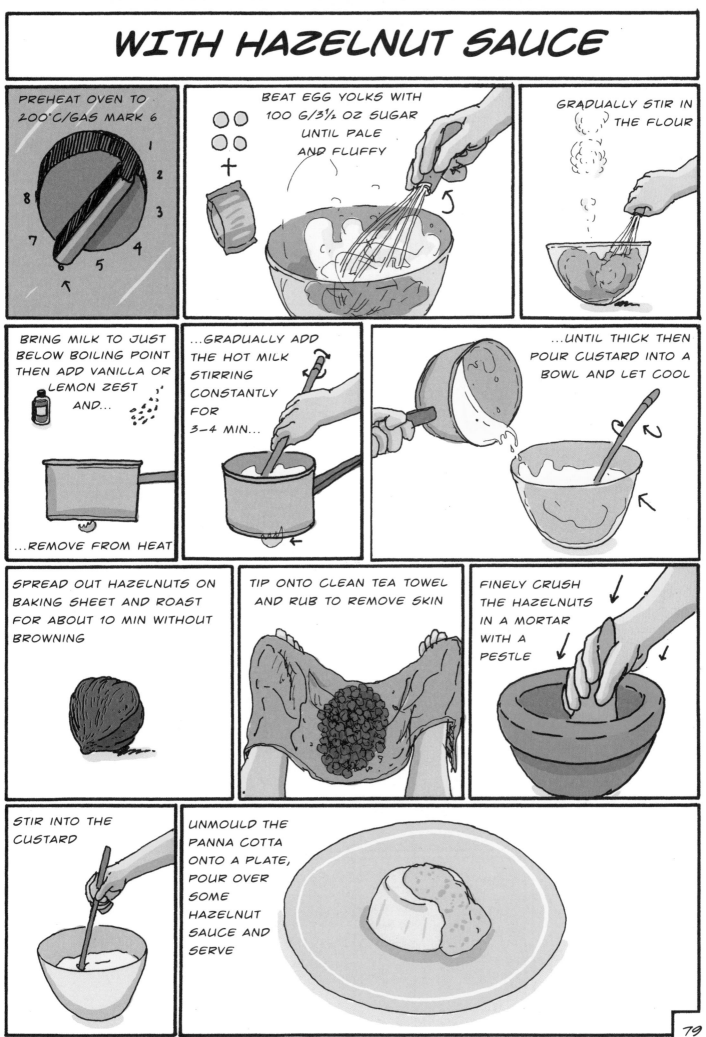

WITH HAZELNUT SAUCE

PREHEAT OVEN TO 200°C/GAS MARK 6

BEAT EGG YOLKS WITH 100 G/3½ OZ SUGAR UNTIL PALE AND FLUFFY

GRADUALLY STIR IN THE FLOUR

BRING MILK TO JUST BELOW BOILING POINT THEN ADD VANILLA OR LEMON ZEST AND...

...REMOVE FROM HEAT

...GRADUALLY ADD THE HOT MILK STIRRING CONSTANTLY FOR 3-4 MIN...

...UNTIL THICK THEN POUR CUSTARD INTO A BOWL AND LET COOL

SPREAD OUT HAZELNUTS ON BAKING SHEET AND ROAST FOR ABOUT 10 MIN WITHOUT BROWNING

TIP ONTO CLEAN TEA TOWEL AND RUB TO REMOVE SKIN

FINELY CRUSH THE HAZELNUTS IN A MORTAR WITH A PESTLE

STIR INTO THE CUSTARD

UNMOULD THE PANNA COTTA ONTO A PLATE, POUR OVER SOME HAZELNUT SAUCE AND SERVE

450 G/1 LB MASCARPONE CHEESE

200 G/7 OZ CASTER SUGAR

30 G/1 OZ CORNFLOUR

120 ML/4 FL OZ SOURED CREAM

1 TSP VANILLA EXTRACT

225 G/8 OZ CREAM CHEESE

½ TSP GRATED LEMON ZEST

4 EGGS

STRAWBERRIES, TO SERVE

MASCARPONE DESSERT

SERVES 6   PREP: 35 MIN, PLUS COOLING   COOK: 40 MIN

PREHEAT OVEN TO 180°C/GAS MARK 4

LINE A 25-CM TIN WITH BAKING PARCHMENT

LEMON ZEST + SUGAR + BOTH CHEESES + VANILLA AND BEAT

When Smooth

GRADUALLY ADD EGGS

SIFT IN CORNFLOUR

THEN BEAT AGAIN

REDUCE HEAT TO 140°C/GAS MARK 1

AND BAKE FOR 1 HR THEN TURN OVEN OFF

LET STAND FOR 1 HR

COOL ON A RACK

Chill

IN FRIDGE FOR 2 HR

SPREAD OVER THIN LAYER SOURED CREAM

SERVE WITH STRAWBERRIES

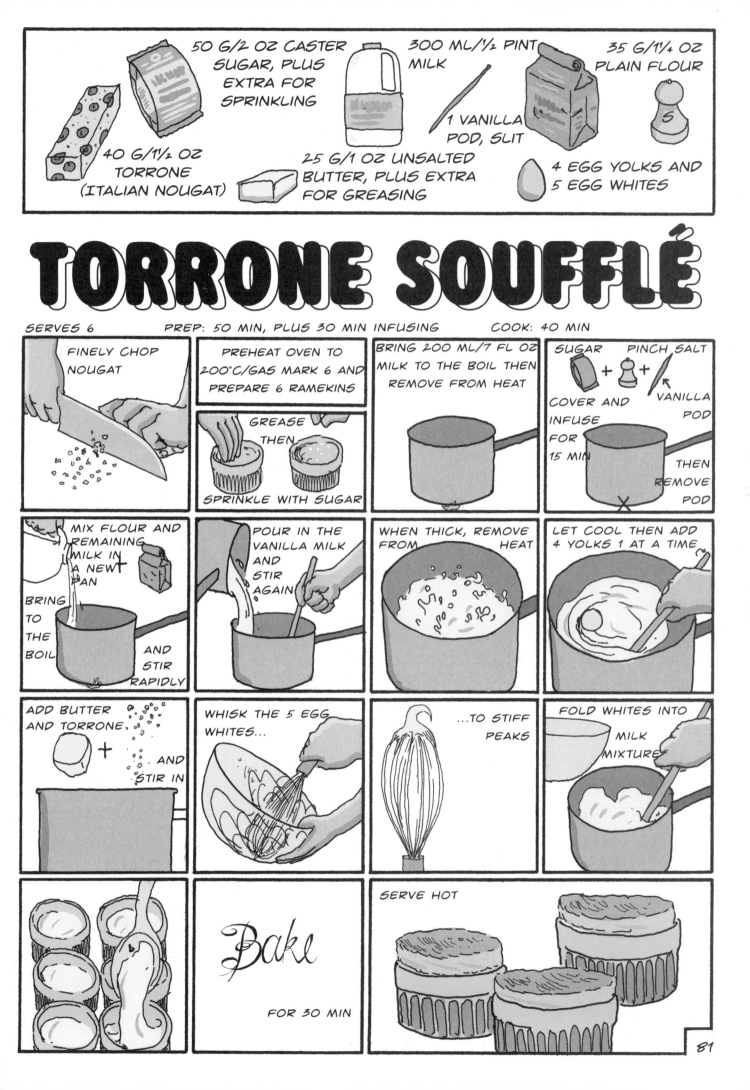

TORRONE SOUFFLÉ

50 G/2 OZ CASTER SUGAR, PLUS EXTRA FOR SPRINKLING

300 ML/½ PINT MILK

35 G/1¼ OZ PLAIN FLOUR

40 G/1½ OZ TORRONE (ITALIAN NOUGAT)

1 VANILLA POD, SLIT

25 G/1 OZ UNSALTED BUTTER, PLUS EXTRA FOR GREASING

4 EGG YOLKS AND 5 EGG WHITES

SERVES 6   PREP: 50 MIN, PLUS 30 MIN INFUSING   COOK: 40 MIN

FINELY CHOP NOUGAT

PREHEAT OVEN TO 200°C/GAS MARK 6 AND PREPARE 6 RAMEKINS

GREASE THEN SPRINKLE WITH SUGAR

BRING 200 ML/7 FL OZ MILK TO THE BOIL THEN REMOVE FROM HEAT

SUGAR + PINCH SALT + VANILLA POD
COVER AND INFUSE FOR 15 MIN THEN REMOVE POD

MIX FLOUR AND REMAINING MILK IN A NEW PAN
BRING TO THE BOIL AND STIR RAPIDLY

POUR IN THE VANILLA MILK AND STIR AGAIN

WHEN THICK, REMOVE FROM HEAT

LET COOL THEN ADD 4 YOLKS 1 AT A TIME

ADD BUTTER AND TORRONE... AND STIR IN

WHISK THE 5 EGG WHITES...

...TO STIFF PEAKS

FOLD WHITES INTO MILK MIXTURE

Bake FOR 30 MIN

SERVE HOT

81

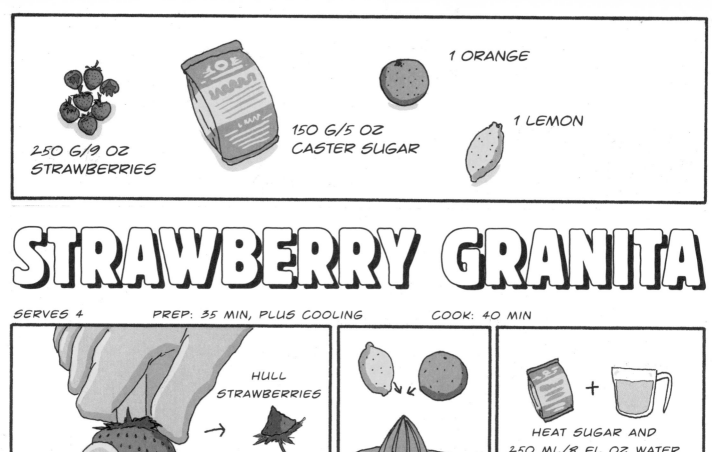

STRAWBERRY GRANITA

SERVES 4   PREP: 35 MIN, PLUS COOLING   COOK: 40 MIN

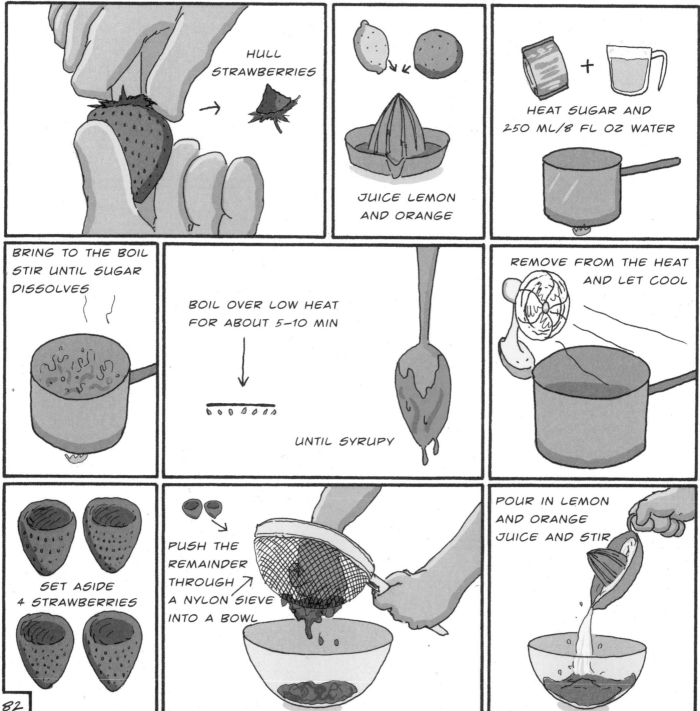

HULL STRAWBERRIES

JUICE LEMON AND ORANGE

HEAT SUGAR AND 250 ML/8 FL OZ WATER

BRING TO THE BOIL STIR UNTIL SUGAR DISSOLVES

BOIL OVER LOW HEAT FOR ABOUT 5–10 MIN

UNTIL SYRUPY

REMOVE FROM THE HEAT AND LET COOL

SET ASIDE 4 STRAWBERRIES

PUSH THE REMAINDER THROUGH A NYLON SIEVE INTO A BOWL

POUR IN LEMON AND ORANGE JUICE AND STIR

ADD THE SYRUP AND STIR

POUR MIXTURE INTO A FREEZERPROOF CONTAINER...

...THEN FREEZE FOR ABOUT 3 HR...

Stir
EVERY 30 MIN

SPOON INTO 4 TALL GLASSES...

...AND DECORATE WITH A STRAWBERRY

FOR AN APRICOT VERSION:

200 G/7 OZ CASTER SUGAR
400 G/14 OZ APRICOTS, PITTED AND CHOPPED
1 TSP VANILLA EXTRACT
JUICE OF 1 LEMON, STRAINED
8 MINT LEAVES

REMOVE FROM HEAT AND LET COOL

THEN PUSH APRICOTS AND SYRUP THROUGH A NYLON SIEVE

BRING SUGAR AND 200 ML/ 7 FL OZ WATER TO THE BOIL AND STIR UNTIL SUGAR DISSOLVES THEN ADD APRICOTS AND SIMMER GENTLY FOR 30 MIN

LOW HEAT

STIR IN VANILLA ESSENCE AND LEMON JUICE

POUR MIXTURE INTO A FREEZERPROOF CONTAINER

FREEZE FOR 3 HR STIRRING EVERY 30 MIN

SPOON INTO 4 TALL GLASSES

AND DECORATE WITH 2 MINT LEAVES

50 G/2 OZ UNSALTED BUTTER, MELTED PLUS EXTRA FOR GREASING

5 EGGS, SEPARATED

VANILLA POD

100 G/3½ OZ PLAIN CHOCOLATE, BROKEN INTO PIECES

20 G/¾ OZ CORNFLOUR

25 G/1 OZ PLAIN FLOUR, PLUS EXTRA FOR DUSTING

25 G/1 OZ CASTER SUGAR

200 G/7 OZ ICING SUGAR

CHOCOLATE DELIGHT

SERVES 4–6   PREP: 50 MIN, PLUS COOLING   COOK: 40 MIN

FOR THE VANILLA SUGAR

VANILLA POD

COVER WITH CASTER SUGAR

SEAL WITH A LID

STORE IN A COOL PLACE FOR 2–3 DAYS BEFORE USING

PREHEAT OVEN TO 150°C/ GAS MARK 2 AND PREPARE A CAKE PAN

DUST... ...WITH FLOUR

MELT BUTTER

LOW HEAT

MELT CHOCOLATE IN HEATPROOF BOWL

MUST NOT TOUCH WATER

BARELY SIMMERING WATER

EGG YOLKS

VANILLA SUGAR + + 100 G/3½ OZ ICING SUGAR

AND BEAT

BEAT IN BUTTER AND CHOCOLATE

SIFT IN FLOUR AND CORNFLOUR AND MIX WELL

84

WHISK EGG WHITES TO STIFF PEAKS

WHISK IN REMAINING ICING SUGAR

GENTLY FOLD IN CHOCOLATE MIXTURE

POUR INTO PREPARED TIN

Bake

FOR 40 MIN

REMOVE FROM OVEN AND COOL ON A WIRE RACK

CUT INTO WEDGES AND SERVE

Chill

IN THE FRIDGE BEFORE TURNING OUT

BLACKBERRY TART

SERVES 6   PREP: 2½ HR   COOK: 45–60 MIN

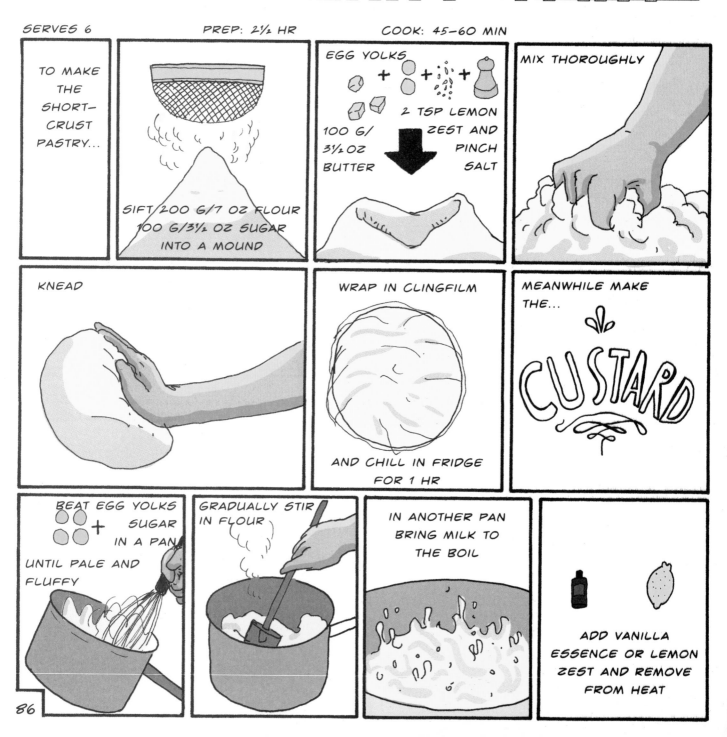

SLOWLY POUR HOT MILK INTO THE EGG MIXTURE AND COOK UNTIL THICKENED, 3–4 MIN

LOW HEAT

POUR INTO A HEATPROOF BOWL AND LET COOL, STIRRING FROM TIME TO TIME

PREHEAT OVEN TO 180°C/GAS MARK 4

GREASE A 27.5–CM TIN

WITH BUTTER

ROLL OUT PASTRY...

...ON A LIGHTLY FLOURED SURFACE

LINE TIN WITH PASTRY AND PRICK BASE WITH A FORK

POUR IN COOLED CUSTARD

Bake

FOR 35–40 MIN

MEANWHILE RESERVE 350 G/2 OZ BLACKBERRIES

PROCESS THE REST

IN A PROCESSOR

BLACKBERRY PUREE + JAM

MIX IN A BOWL

REMOVE TART FROM OVEN AND LET COOL ON WIRE RACK

SPREAD BLACKBERRY MIXTURE OVER THE BAKED CUSTARD

...AND SERVE

TOP WITH RESERVED BLACKBERRIES

87

500 G/1 LB 2 OZ FRUITS OF THE FOREST

3 EGG YOLKS

65 G/2½ OZ CASTER SUGAR

½ LEMON

2 TBSP GRAND MARNIER

(SUCH AS STRAWBERRIES, BLACKBERRIES, RASPBERRIES, BLUEBERRIES)

FOREST FRUITS WITH ZABAGLIONE

SERVES 4   PREP: 20 MIN   COOK: 30 MIN

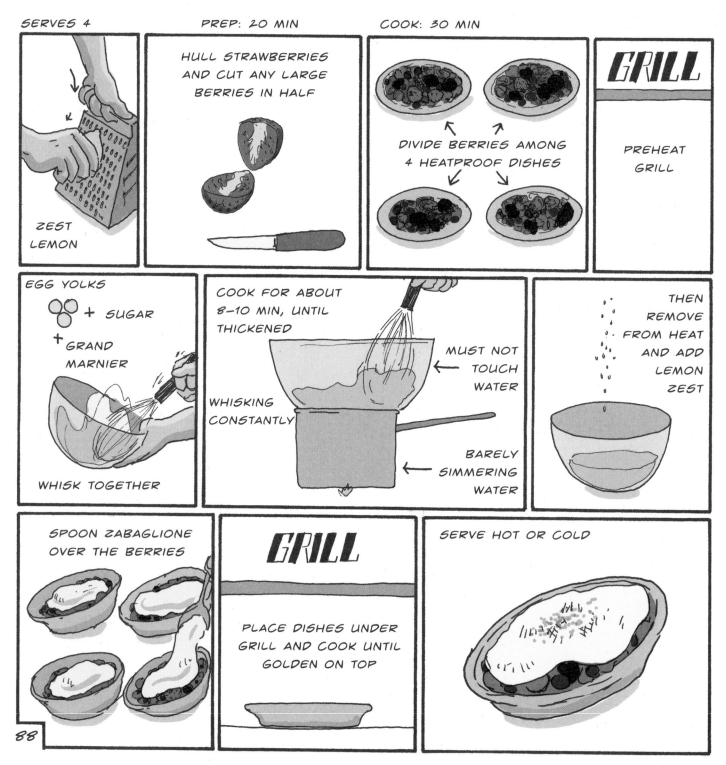

ZEST LEMON

HULL STRAWBERRIES AND CUT ANY LARGE BERRIES IN HALF

DIVIDE BERRIES AMONG 4 HEATPROOF DISHES

GRILL

PREHEAT GRILL

EGG YOLKS + SUGAR + GRAND MARNIER

WHISK TOGETHER

COOK FOR ABOUT 8–10 MIN, UNTIL THICKENED

WHISKING CONSTANTLY

MUST NOT TOUCH WATER

BARELY SIMMERING WATER

THEN REMOVE FROM HEAT AND ADD LEMON ZEST

SPOON ZABAGLIONE OVER THE BERRIES

GRILL

PLACE DISHES UNDER GRILL AND COOK UNTIL GOLDEN ON TOP

SERVE HOT OR COLD

5 YELLOW PEACHES

25 G/1 OZ UNSALTED BUTTER, PLUS EXTRA FOR GREASING

50 G/2 OZ CASTER SUGAR

2 EGG YOLKS

25 G/1 OZ COCOA POWDER

4 AMARETTI BISCUITS, CRUSHED

STUFFED PEACHES

SERVES 4   PREP: 20 MIN   COOK: 30 MIN

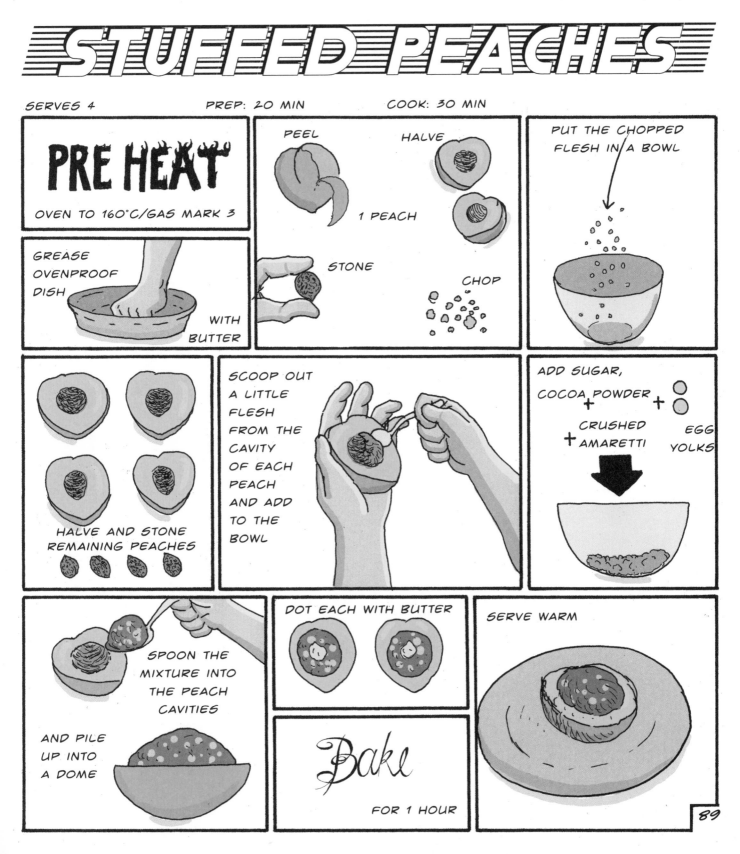

PRE HEAT

OVEN TO 160°C/GAS MARK 3

GREASE OVENPROOF DISH WITH BUTTER

PEEL   HALVE

1 PEACH

STONE   CHOP

PUT THE CHOPPED FLESH IN A BOWL

HALVE AND STONE REMAINING PEACHES

SCOOP OUT A LITTLE FLESH FROM THE CAVITY OF EACH PEACH AND ADD TO THE BOWL

ADD SUGAR, COCOA POWDER + CRUSHED AMARETTI + EGG YOLKS

SPOON THE MIXTURE INTO THE PEACH CAVITIES

AND PILE UP INTO A DOME

DOT EACH WITH BUTTER

Bake

FOR 1 HOUR

SERVE WARM

2–3 TBSP WHITE RUM

150 G/5 OZ PLAIN FLOUR, PLUS EXTRA FOR DUSTING

1 TBSP LARD

1 EGG WHITE, PLUS EXTRA FOR BRUSHING

1 TSP CASTER SUGAR

2 TSP WHITE WINE VINEGAR

1 KG/2¼ LB RICOTTA ROMANA

400 G/14 OZ ICING SUGAR, PLUS EXTRA FOR DUSTING

VEGETABLE OIL, FOR FRYING

4–5 PISTACHIOS, SLIVERED

80 G/3 OZ CHOCOLATE, CHOPPED

¾ TBSP MALVASIA WINE

50 G/2 OZ CANDIED PUMPKIN, DICED

CANNOLI

MAKES 20–22   PREP: 30 MIN, PLUS STANDING   COOK: 1 HR

Filling

PIPING BAG

PRESS RICOTTA THROUGH SIEVE INTO A BOWL

ADD ICING SUGAR AND BEAT

WITH A WOODEN SPOON

PUMPKIN + CHOCOLATE + RUM

MIX WELL

COVER WITH CLINGFILM AND CHILL IN REFRIGERATOR FOR 12 HR

DOUGH

SIFT FLOUR + PINCH SALT

ADD LARD, VINEGAR, WINE (OPTIONAL) EGG WHITE, CASTER SUGAR, MIX WELL UNTIL FIRM

SHAPE INTO A BALL

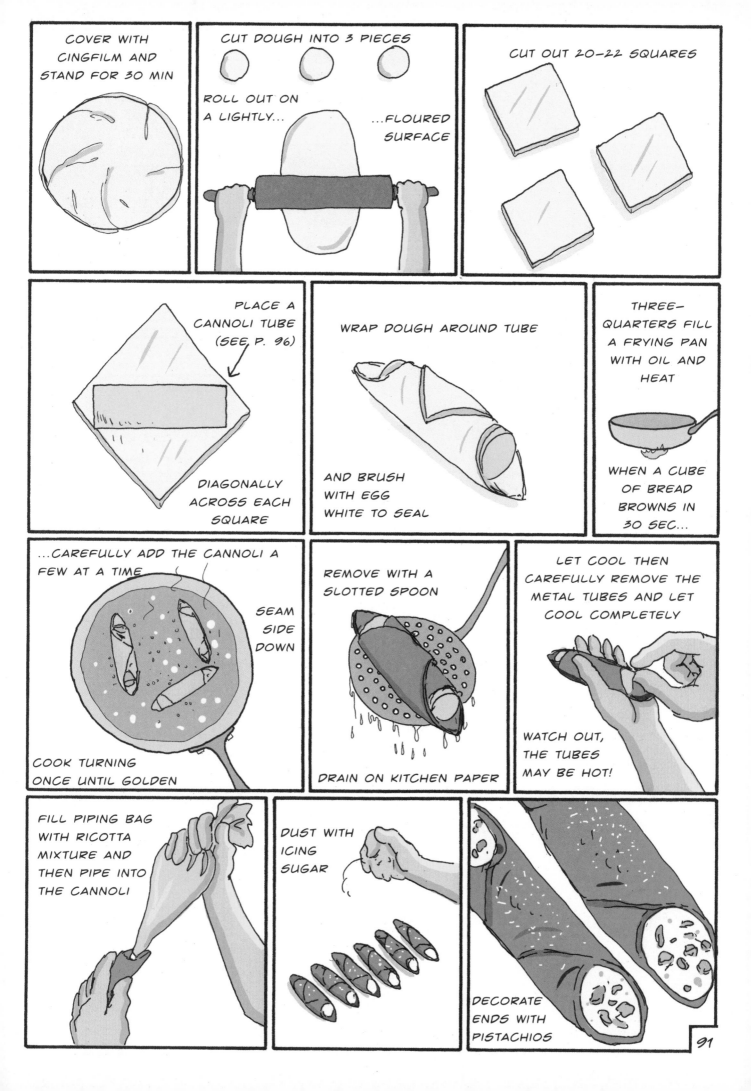

COVER WITH CINGFILM AND STAND FOR 30 MIN

CUT DOUGH INTO 3 PIECES

ROLL OUT ON A LIGHTLY...

...FLOURED SURFACE

CUT OUT 20-22 SQUARES

PLACE A CANNOLI TUBE (SEE P. 96)

SEE P. 96

DIAGONALLY ACROSS EACH SQUARE

WRAP DOUGH AROUND TUBE

AND BRUSH WITH EGG WHITE TO SEAL

THREE-QUARTERS FILL A FRYING PAN WITH OIL AND HEAT

WHEN A CUBE OF BREAD BROWNS IN 30 SEC...

...CAREFULLY ADD THE CANNOLI A FEW AT A TIME

SEAM SIDE DOWN

COOK TURNING ONCE UNTIL GOLDEN

REMOVE WITH A SLOTTED SPOON

DRAIN ON KITCHEN PAPER

LET COOL THEN CAREFULLY REMOVE THE METAL TUBES AND LET COOL COMPLETELY

WATCH OUT, THE TUBES MAY BE HOT!

FILL PIPING BAG WITH RICOTTA MIXTURE AND THEN PIPE INTO THE CANNOLI

DUST WITH ICING SUGAR

DECORATE ENDS WITH PISTACHIOS

91

RECIPE NOTES

Butter should always be unsalted.

Herbs are always fresh, unless otherwise specified.

Pepper is always freshly ground black pepper, unless otherwise specified.

Eggs, vegetables and fruits are assumed to be medium size, unless otherwise specified.

Milk is always whole, unless otherwise specified.

Garlic cloves are assumed to be large; use two if yours are small.

Ham means cooked ham, unless otherwise specified.

A number of the recipes include alcohol, which can easily be replaced with water, stock or, if a dessert, orange juice.

Prosciutto refers exclusively to raw, dry-cured ham, usually from Parma or San Daniele in northern Italy.

Cooking and preparation times are for guidance only, as individual ovens vary. If using a fan oven, follow the manufacturer's instructions concerning oven temperatures.

To test whether your deep-frying oil is hot enough, add a cube of stale bread. If it browns in thirty seconds, the temperature is 180–190°C, about right for most frying. Exercise caution when deep frying: add the food carefully to avoid splashing, wear long sleeves, and never leave the pan unattended.

Some recipes include raw or very lightly cooked eggs. These should be avoided particularly by the elderly, infants, pregnant women, convalescents, and anyone with an impaired immune system.

All spoon measurements are level. 1 teaspoon = 5 ml; 1 tablespoon = 15 ml. Australian standard tablespoons are 20 ml, so Australian readers are advised to use 3 teaspoons in place of 1 tablespoon when measuring small quantities.

Metric and imperial measurements are given throughout. Follow one set of measurements, not a mixture, as they are not interchangeable.

TECHNIQUES IN DETAIL

FISH (DE-SCALE & CLEAN)

Scrape off the scales of a fish by working from tail to head, using the back of a knife. Trim away the fins. Insert the point of your knife in the belly button (about two-thirds along) and cut along the belly. Scoop out the entrails with your hand. Rinse.

KNEAD

Pushing, pulling and folding dough over itself for several minutes to work in air and make it elastic. Best done on a lightly floured surface. Alternatively, an electric stand mixer fitted with a dough hook may be used. Pasta and yeast doughs are kneaded vigorously, whereas pastry dough is kneaded lightly and only briefly.

MUSSELS (CLEAN & PREP)

Scrub the mussels hard under running water with a scourer or knife to remove any barnacles. Pull away the hairy bit known as the 'beard'. Rinse well. The shells should be closed. If there are open shells, tap them – they will close if they are still alive. If a shell does not close, discard it.

PRAWNS (PREP)

It's not essential to devein prawns (removing the dark vein that runs along the back) but the vein can be gritty and unpleasant to eat. Remove the head from the body and peel the body shell away. Cut along the back with a sharp knife just far enough in to reveal the vein, then pull this out and discard it.

SARDINES (SCALE, CLEAN & BONE)

Scrape off the scales from tail to head with the back of a knife (see De-scale & Clean Fish). Supporting the back of the fish with your free hand, insert the tip of the knife at the tail end and run it up the length of the body. Remove and discard the guts and rinse well. Pull away the gills and rinse the fish to remove the blood line. Turn the fish on its back, and with your finger, gently loosen the bones close to the backbone and release the fine bones away from the flesh. Lift up the bone and using scissors, snip the bone at the tail end and discard. Remove any remaining pin bones with tweezers.

SQUID (PREP)

Squid is often sold cleaned and prepared. If not, they are simple to clean and prepare at home. Hold the squid head in one hand and the tentacles in another. Pull firmly to separate. Cut the tentacles away from the intestine just below the eye of the squid and remove the soft skeleton (beak) at the centre of the tentacles. Rinse.

WHISK/BEAT

Mixing with a balloon or electric whisk, handheld mixer or an electric stand mixer to make ingredients such as eggs, butter or cream light and frothy. If whisking egg whites, especially for a soufflé, do be sure to use a clean, dry bowl.

GLOSSARY

AL DENTE
Essential Italian term for cooking pasta until tender but still firm to the bite.

BAKE IN A PARCEL
Wrapping fish, meat or vegetables in a pocket of aluminium foil or baking paper to keep it moist during cooking.

BAKING BEANS
Pea-sized, ceramic beans used to line uncooked pastry cases for pre-cooking.

BATON
Vegetables cut into long, thin, rectangular sticks, about the diameter of a pencil.

BÉCHAMEL
A white sauce made using a roux (a paste) of equal parts butter and flour, then whisking in milk over the heat until you get a thick, creamy sauce.

BLANCH
Briefly plunging fruit or vegetables into boiling water to soften but not completely cook them.

BLEND
Whizzing together ingredients in an electric blender or food processor until creamy or chopped to a pulp.

BOIL
Cooking ingredients for a specified length of time in water or stock that is bubbling vigorously.

BOLOGNESE
Meaning 'from the city of Bologna', it can refer to any dish from that region such as ragú (meat sauce), tagliatelle or lasagne.

BREAD/BREADCRUMBS
Dipping fish, meat or vegetables in whisked egg, then in breadcrumbs, before frying until crisp and golden.

BROWN IN AN OVEN
Popping something like lasagne into a hot oven for five to ten minutes until it's golden brown, and bubbling on top.

BROWN IN A PAN
Cooking meat or vegetables (like garlic or onions) in butter or oil over medium heat until they are golden and shimmering.

BRUSCHETTA
A slice of lightly toasted, stale bread rubbed with garlic, drizzled with oil, and most commonly topped with chopped tomatoes.

CACCIATORE
A 'hunter's style' one-pot casserole of chicken or rabbit cooked with onions and mushrooms, or tomatoes, peppers and carrots.

CANNOLI TUBE
Tubes around which cannoli dough is wrapped before deep frying. Usually made of metal, they are available to buy from good kitchenware stores.

CAPONATA

Sicilian *antipasto* of diced aubergines, peppers and tomatoes slowly stewed in a sweet-and-sour sauce of vinegar, raisins and capers.

CARVE

Slicing roast meat with a long, sharp knife, using a long-handled, two-pronged fork to hold it steady. Easiest if the meat has been left to stand for ten to fifteen minutes after it comes out of the oven.

CHOP

Chopping ingredients into bite-sized chunks.

COCOTTE

Cooking something slowly in a thick porcelain or terracotta pot covered by a lid.

COOK OVER LOW HEAT

Getting something meltingly tender by turning the heat to its lowest setting and cooking for a long time.

COOK UNTIL SOFTENED

Usually applies to vegetables such as onions that need to be cooked down until soft, sweet and translucent.

COVER

Placing a lid over the top of a pan or dish to seal in moisture and stop ingredients from drying out.

COVER WITH A THIN LAYER

Just covering the contents of a dish with a thin layer of cream, gelatine or sauce.

CRUSH

Smashing garlic with the back of a knife, or grinding spices in a pestle and mortar.

CUT INTO PORTIONS

Dividing meat, poultry or fish into one-person-sized pieces.

DE-SEED

Scraping out and discarding the seeds from, for example, a red pepper or chilli.

DEEP FRY

Bringing a pan of fat or oil (vegetable is best) to a boil for deep frying. Add a cube of stale bread. If it browns in thirty seconds, the oil is ready.

DUST WITH FLOUR

Lightly coating ingredients with flour before frying to make them crunchier.

EVAPORATE

Allowing excess liquid to bubble off a sauce in order to thicken it.

FILL

Stuffing pastry shells with, for example, eggs or fruit, or layering cakes with cream or jam.

FOLD

Gently mixing flour with cutting movements into liquids (eggs and sugar) with a stainless steel spoon or knife.

GARNISH

The final decoration before a dish is served. Herbs, lemon slices and salad are common examples.

GREASE

Rubbing oil, butter or fat into a baking tin or mould to stop a mixture sticking when you cook it.

MALVASIA WINE

A group of wine grape varieties grown in the Mediterranean. The sweet variety is used in desserts, such as Cannoli (p. 90–91). Maderia may be used as an altenative.

MASCARPONE

A creamy, fresh Italian cheese from the Lombardy region, similar to cream cheese, but with a tangy and nutty flavour. Most often used for desserts, such as Tiramisu (p. 77).

MILANESE

Fillets or chops of chicken or veal (occasionally vegetables) breaded and sautéed in butter until crisp.

MORTAR & PESTLE

Utensils used for grinding spices or pounding pesto to a paste. A blender can be used instead.

MOUND

Sifting flour directly onto a counter into a pyramid shape for making pasta.

PANCETTA

Cured, salted or smoked pork belly, great for flavouring the base of sauces.

PASSATA

Canned, crushed and sieved tomatoes (less concentrated than tomato purée).

POLENTA

Ground corn that can be served like a mash or set into wedges and baked or grilled.

PORCINI

Large, brown-cap mushrooms with lots of flesh and little gill.

POUND

Softening meat or vegetable fibres by battering them with something heavy such as a meat mallet or a rolling pin.

PRE HEAT

Bringing the oven to a specified temperature before you start cooking.

PROSCIUTTO

Cured ham, the best of which comes from Parma.

RIBOLLITA

Meaning 'reboiled'. A warming Tuscan stew based on cavolo nero (Tuscan cabbage) and white beans, usually reheated and eaten the day after making.

RICOTTA ROMANA

An Italian curd cheese made from the whey from whole sheep's milk. It has a rich but delicate flavour that is sweeter than other types of ricotta.

SALSA VERDE

Tangy green sauce of capers and herbs for serving with grilled fish or meat.

SEMIFREDDO

Quick-to-make, partially frozen, soft ice cream.

SHRED

Finely cutting ingredients like cabbage and lettuce into thin strips.

SIMMER

Bringing liquid down to just below boiling point or to turn down the heat under a liquid that has reached boiling point so that the surface of the liquid barely ripples.

SOAK
Softening dried fruits, vegetables or funghi such as mushrooms in water to plump up before cooking.

SPRINKLE
Adding one lot of ingredients slowly to another, or scattering an ingredient over a surface.

STIR IN BUTTER OR CREAM
Adding butter or cream at the end of a dish to give a rich, velvety and shiny finish.

STUFF
Putting savoury ingredients like rice or breadcrumbs into another ingredient, such as hollowed-out tomatoes or chicken.

TALEGGIO
Named after Val Taleggio in northern Italy, this soft, creamy cheese has a strong aroma but a mild, fruity flavour.

TIE MEAT
Wrapping meat in butchers' string to hold in shape while cooking.

YEAST, FRESH/DRY
For rising bread dough or other baked goods. Note that while dried yeast can be added directly to flour, fresh yeast needs first to be mixed with water.

MENU IDEAS

SPRING MENU

Grilled Stuffed Squid, p. 17

·

Potato & Spinach Gnocchi,
p. 39

·

Chicken Stuffed with
Mascarpone, pp. 54–55

·

Panna Cottawith
Hazelnut Sauce, pp. 78–79

SUMMER MENU

Tomato Bruschetta, p. 22

·

Linguine with Pesto, p. 46

·

Sea Bass Baked
in a Parcel, p. 62

·

Cannoli, pp. 90–91

AUTUMN MENU

Stuffed Porcini
Mushrooms, pp. 14–15

·

Tagliatelle with
Peas & Ham, p. 38

·

Slow-Cooked Tuna, p. 63

·

Apple Cake, p. 76

WINTER MENU

Ribollita, p. 28

·

Cheese & Vegetable
Filled Ravioli, pp. 44–45

·

Chicken Cacciatore,
p. 60

·

Tiramisu, p. 77

QUICK WEEKNIGHT SUPPER

Eggs en Cocotte,
p. 19

·

Fusilli with
Mushrooms, p. 40

·

Forest Fruits
with Zabaglione, p. 88

LIGHT LUNCH

Spinach Salad
with Bacon & Beans,
p. 31

·

Mussels Marinara,
p. 53

·

Strawberry or Apricot
Granita, pp. 82–83

BIRTHDAY DINNER

Pizza Marghertia,
pp. 21–22

·

Farfalle with
Prawns, p. 47

·

Grilled Sardines, p. 58

·

Stuffed Peaches,
p. 89

DINING AL FRESCO

Panzanella, p. 30

·

Rigatoni with
Meatballs, p. 42

·

Fritto Misto, pp. 66–67

·

Raspberry
Semifreddo, p. 75

Phaidon Press Limited
Regent's Wharf
All Saints Street
London N1 9PA

www.phaidon.com

First published 2014
© 2014 Phaidon Press Limited

ISBN: 978 0 7148 6746 5
(UK Edition)

Chop, Sizzle, Wow originates from Il cucchiaio d'argento,
first published in 1950, eighth edition (revised, expanded
and updated in 1997), and Il cucchiaio d'argento estate, first
published in 2005. © Editoriale Domus S.p.a

A CIP catalogue record for this book is available from
the British Library.

Commissioning Editors: Emma Robertson
& Emilia Terragni
Project Editor: Sophie Hodgkin
Production Controller: Adela Cory

Introduction by Tara Stevens
Inked Illustrations by Adriano de Campos Rampazzo
Illustration colour by Colin White
Design by Julia Hasting
Layout by Hans Stofregen & Colin White

Printed in Romania